Dev on the Spectrum

The True Story of a Boy Who Changed Lives

Kent Winter

INDIA · SINGAPORE · MALAYSIA

Notion Press

No. 8, 3rd Cross Street
CIT Colony, Mylapore
Chennai, Tamil Nadu – 600004

First Published by Notion Press 2021
Copyright © Kent Winter 2021
All Rights Reserved.

ISBN 978-1-63806-653-8

CONTENTS

———

PREFACE

Hi. My name is Kent. I've been married to the woman of my dreams, Donna, since 1990 and we have two sons, Kullen, who was born in 1992, and Devin, who was born in 1995. Our sons are both fantastic young men.

Kullen graduated from college with a criminal justice degree in 2019 and started his career in that field in 2020. He's much like me – into sports, rock music, shooting pool, wakeboarding and working out. He also has my fear of heights, which he began to overcome when he started rock climbing in 2019.

This book, though, is focused on Devin, whose life tragically ended in 2019, after a life of suffering inside, while appearing happy on the outside. Devin had autism but also a host of other issues you will come to understand as you read through this book.

Devin and I talked a couple times about writing a book about his life, sort of an autobiography that I would help with, maybe as in interview where I would prompt him, then get text in his exact words to create the chapters. You'll see, as you read through this book, why his exact words would be so important. He came up with the title of this book.

As you'll see, Devin developed a fondness for poetry. Donna and I considered creating a book simply called *Devin's Poems*.

I decided to combine the two book ideas into a single, biographical book about his life, so you can get to know him, appreciate all he went through, and have that background context as you read his poetry. I believe you will find from reading this book that he was truly a one of a kind person, always kind and loving, respectful, never judgmental, always honest and loyal, and appreciative of the beautiful world around him. He was also quite the daredevil…

ACKNOWLEDGEMENTS

———

I would like to thank my wife, Donna, for helping me capture all the memories and for helping proofread the early revisions. Most of all, though, for sticking with me all these years. I would not be the person I am without her, and am not sure I would have survived this horrible loss without her by my side.

I would also like to thank Rob Bignell at Inventing Reality Editing Service for his expert advice, and my friend and long-time business associate and co-worker, Kishen Kavikondala, for so graciously offering to handle the publishing of this book.

And finally, I would like to thank Team Devin, a core group of people, some family, and some friends, who spent countless hours in ICU with us in Devin's final two weeks. Here they are, in no particular order – Darren, Celine, Josh, Tim, Ashley, Jerry, Brad, Chad, Jeff, Tracy, Debbie, Mark, Kyle, Lindsey, Steve, Matt, Kullen, Liz, Gary, Kelly, Dave, Kelly, Lou and Shannon. We would not have made it through this without you all.

Chapter 1

THE EARLY YEARS

There have been two times in my life that an image was so vivid in my dreams that I knew it had to be real. I'll explain one of them now, the other much later in the book.

When I was about 14, I had this dream where I had a ring, and when I would touch it, this incredible woman would appear. She was petite, with long curly hair, fair skin and crystal eyes. She was always moving along trails in the woods, and I could never quite catch up to her, but I could see her, plain as day. It was one of those dreams that felt incredibly real, to the point I woke up looking for the ring. A few years later I took a student-work job, part of the financial aid program, at the print shop at the Junior College in Belleville, Illinois. My first day on the job I bumped into this beautiful girl, the one from the dream, who had also just started working there.

We became friends right away, and it grew into much more. As we moved on from the print shop, I was working in a small factory in Belleville, and taking classes at Washington University in St. Louis. Donna was working for a bank in downtown St. Louis. She would meet my mom at the K-Mart in west Belleville, and ride the Bi-

State bus together. We bought a small, like 900 square feet, house in Mascoutah, just behind Donna's childhood home, where her mom, Jan, and step-dad, John, lived. We didn't have much, but we had family nearby and got to spend lots of time with our great friends, Dave and Kelly. We dated for a couple years, and then married in 1990, and had our first child, Kullen in 1992, before I graduated college in 1993.

I earned a mechanical engineering degree, but at the time, the St Louis market was flooded with engineers, as Boeing had been downsizing. After months of job hunting, we decided to accept an opportunity with Orscheln Company in central Missouri, in one of their automotive supply plants in Salisbury. We packed up and moved to a small pink rental house in Moberly in September 1993. Donna was offered a transfer to continue working with Boatmen's bank, where she had been for several years at their location in downtown St Louis, as a fleet-leasing originator, but we could not find a daycare we were comfortable with. After much deliberation, Donna decided to run a daycare in our home, as her mom, Jan, had done throughout Donna's entire childhood.

Our life was simple. It was good. Moberly was a nice family community but was left somewhat deprived when DuPont pulled out of town after a union strike some years before we moved there. We spent lots of time playing outside, going to the nice parks, especially for fireworks over the lake on Independence Day, and taking trips to Columbia, to see big events like Disney on Ice at the university or one of the public events venues.

Contrary to common practice, at least where we came from in Belleville, Illinois, the practice in Moberly, Missouri, was to allow Sudafed and other medicines during pregnancy, and also to accelerate delivery by pushing down on mom's stomach to get the water to break. Devin Mitchell Winter was born in May 1995, a perfect, green-eyed, blond-haired baby, about 5 weeks early, all six pounds, two ounces of him. Aside from jaundice, he was good to go. Kullen, then two-and-a-half-years-old, could not have been happier to welcome Devin home.

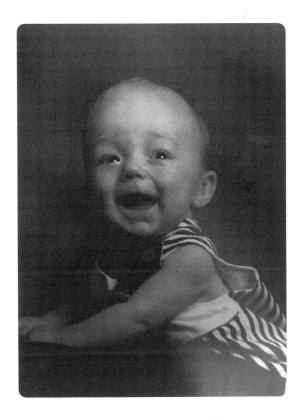

Devin at three months old

Grandma Jan holding Devin when he was one year old

Kullen and Devin

We survived some tornadoes while living in Moberly. One hit while we were in an arena in Columbia, with the kids, seeing Barney live on stage. The power went out, and the whole crowd freaked out. The most serious, though, was in 1995. I was out in the yard, and Donna called out that the TV said a tornado was coming. Our house had no basement, and there was no storm shelter I knew of in town, so I did the math, and realized we had time to get across town to our friends, the Crawford's house where they had a basement. As we drove across town in our teal and silver Chevy Astro van, we could see the tornado in the distance behind us. Mark and Sharon welcomed us in, and we listened to the storm on the radio. The storm ripped through and left a path diagonally across town, skipping over our house. There were lots of uprooted trees and flipped vehicles. Roofs were torn off, and debris landed as far as Quincy, Illinois, about 90 miles away. The good news was we were all safe, and our house sustained no damage.

About a year after we moved to Moberly, I learned that Orscheln intended to close the plant in Salisbury. I was assigned the project of transferring some of the production to a facility in Hannibal, and the rest to our joint-venture plant in Columbia. I completed this project and then was faced with the decision to work in Hannibal or Columbia. We chose Columbia because it would not force an immediate relocation, and I could continue classes toward my master's degree at the University of Missouri.

After a few months, we decided to move to Columbia. The commute was only about 45 minutes most days, but was on two-lane roads, and made for very long days including the time in the office. We moved from our pink house in Moberly to a duplex on the north side of Columbia. The location was nice. It was about 30 minutes closer to family, it was close to some nice parks and some good preschools, and it was in a location that allowed the Crawfords to continue having Donna as their daycare provider. The duplex sat on a hill, and had a nice fenced back yard. It was spacious, and in pretty good shape. The only real downfall was that as we were moving in, we noticed fleas and roaches, and the place had to be treated multiple times to remove them.

The duplex was a split-level with the garage and a big family room downstairs, and the kitchen, living room and bedrooms upstairs. The winters are fairly rough in that part of the country, and the driveway sloped down to the north making snow and ice removal difficult, so lots of rock-salt and other ice-melt compounds were used. Devin was able to crawl up and down the stairs, but sometimes would stop at the landing in the middle, where there was a combination of bug sprays and ice-melt compounds on the floor, and those hands would make it to his mouth on occasion before we could get to him to clean them.

Devin developed a fever and was crying for what seemed like weeks after he received his normal battery of 18-month immunizations. He was miserable all through

Christmas that year, crying while Donna helped him open presents. We noticed a couple other things – he stopped saying "momma" and was no longer looking us in the eyes when we talked to him. Our pediatrician said we should start to look into autism, as it was likely he had it. We questioned if it could have been caused by the immunizations, the bug sprays or the rock salt, and the answer was no, it just happens.

At that time, autism occurred in approximately one in every 500 children, and while there was ongoing research, there was, and still is, no known cause. At the time of this writing, in 2020, autism occurs in one out of every 59 children. Some of this radical increase is likely better diagnosis, but regardless, it is devastating, and is increasing in frequency at an alarming rate.

While doctors will say immunizations don't cause it, the CDC did require the removal of Thiomersal, a mercury-based preservative in 2001[A]. Regardless the cause, we were faced with the horrible reality that he might never speak, there was no way to know how far he could go, as in some cases, speech never returns, and children end up permanently disabled. As this significant news set-in, we decided to find a job near home to get back closer to family in southern Illinois.

An opportunity came up with A.O. Smith in Granite City, Illinois, about 40 miles from Mascoutah, Donna's hometown, so we jumped on it. Not long after starting there, Tower Automotive completed its acquisition of A.O. Smith's automotive division. Tower was a great fit for me, as my personal approach to life, work and business aligned perfectly with their mission, vision, values and goals. We moved back into our little white house in Mascoutah that we had rented to Dave and Kelly while we were living in Missouri.

Devin had prototypical autism, that is, a delay in his ability to communicate verbally, for two and a half years in his case, combined with discomfort around loud noises, and intolerance to certain types of foods and textures. During his non-verbal years, he developed the typical arm-flapping and archers-bowing, and would jump up and down when really excited or when something was really funny. His "eeeee" noises became commonplace around our home and our extended family. He could laugh at funny things, like when his brother would jump on the bed and do flips, but he could not talk. When he laughed, everyone around the room had to laugh, as he would jump around or rock back and forth in his chair; you could see and feel the excitement. As a parent of a child with autism, one of the hardest things to watch is the child yearning for friendship, but not really having the capacity to have it. It is quite common to see your child outside the circle of kids having fun, watching them, and smiling, but not playing along.

Devin and Kullen shared a room. I would lay in bed next to Devin every night to help him get to sleep. We would make up silly stories. The show *Rugrats* had a name for bigfoot; the kids on the show called him Satchmo. One night we were talking about this, and it turned in to us all singing what we called Satchmo songs. "Hey, wudda you know, Satchmo…can't build a snowman without no snow Satchmo." Devin would belly laugh at all the different rhymes we came up with. Another favorite jingle was "Moto Kitty," a spoof of the Megadeth song "Motopsycho" with a backstory we made up about a kid who had a kitten with no back legs, so he duct-taped the kitty to a powered skateboard, and the kitty could race around the driveway.

We also used to play a game we called "get up on there." I would lay across the bed on my stomach. Kullen would pile on, in same orientation, then Devin would climb up on top. I would start bouncing then toss them left or right. Then I'd yell "get up on there" and it would start again. Devin would play for hours if my back could handle it.

I cannot possibly overstate how much Kullen and Devin loved each other. They were best buds. Kullen was a great big brother, always looking out for Devin, playing with him, and including him as part of the gang when his friends would come over.

As a parent of a child with autism, it's important to separate the fact that they can't communicate verbally from the fact that they can interact, can love, and can make decisions. It just requires the neuro-typical people around them to think differently, employ different strategies, and be patient. I sometimes struggled with the latter. My jobs have always been stressful, and Devin could sense this and would assume I was upset with him. This caused added stress and anxiety on him.

When Devin was about two and a half, I was on a business trip in Chicago, and Donna called me in a panic as she had gotten results from some tests we had done the week before, and there was a chance Devin had leukemia. I rushed home and we went to the hospital together. His symptoms were enlarged lymph glands, visible from across the room in the back of his neck, but also all up and down his torso and pelvic area, visible by scans. He also had an enlarged spleen and liver.

In an attempt to diagnose the condition, many tests were required, including a bone marrow biopsy, a spinal tap, and an MRI, to name a few. Since he could not speak, we couldn't tell if he understood, so he had to be restrained to give him whatever sedatives or other things might be required. This usually required a nose tube, as he would scream and spit out anything we tried to get him to drink. After a few events, we began to cocoon him in blankets so he couldn't kick or grab, as they were administering medications. The doctors also started giving him a little Versed in his drink while we were in the waiting room. This really calmed him down. The result of the series of tests was that they found antibodies in his spinal fluid that may have caused some brain damage, possibly leading to the autistic characteristics – a possible link to something that may cause autism.

A team of seven experts including Dr. Shenoy at St Louis Children's Hospital worked together, and with the help of a new doctor in town, from Boston, Dr. Chatila, determined what he had was Autoimmune Lymphoproliferative Syndrome (ALPS), an extremely rare genetic disorder[B] that had just begun to be diagnosed in 1995 with the discovery of the FAS gene mutation[C]. At that time, Devin was the thirteenth person in the world to have it, and the doctor from Boston had seen it before. To me, there is no way this was a coincidence. The odds are just too great. A recent update about this disorder indicates that there are about 300 families globally, or 500 people, dealing with it[D].

ALPS doesn't allow lymph cells to die like normal. Rather, they proliferate, swelling glands and enlarging the liver and spleen. The treatment for ALPS is a steroid regimen. The steroids give the lymph cells an avenue to die as they should. The prognosis was that we should not expect him to live to be an old man, as they expected things like lymphoma as he would get older. We would have to start him on a high dose of a steroid to get the process started, then he would need to remain on a maintenance dose for life. Devin would need blood tests every 6 to 12 months to ensure the dose of steroid was sufficient to keep the ALPS in check.

The interesting thing with Devin's case was that when we began treatment to get his ALPS in line, we saw a decrease in his autistic tendencies. This led the team at Children's Hospital to document the potential link between his autoimmune condition and autism in their Journal of Pediatrics report in 2010[E].

When they diagnosed him with ALPS, they asked if they could do some research on me and Donna, as the disease was so rare. Children's Hospital is part of the Washington University Medical Center, one of the best around for such research. We agreed but decided that we didn't want to know which of us was the carrier, as we didn't want to live in fear. Looking back, at that point we should have dedicated a significant portion of our resources – time, money, etc. – to better understanding ALPS and what can be done to improve and extend the lives of those inflicted.

The unfortunate thing about introductory high-dose steroids is they cause significant swelling, especially in the face, along with insomnia, weight gain, and irritability. When given at the time a child is non-verbal, this makes for a tough combination. Devin was miserable and so was crying all the time. The good news was that the high-dose was only required for a couple weeks, then over a series of months, we backed it down to a very low dose, and eventually got it down to an every-other-day dose, so small that most doctors will argue it cannot have a benefit.

The Mascoutah School District had a lot to offer for special needs back then. When Devin was three years old, he was accepted to the early childhood program at Scott Air Force Base, with Mr. Simon as his teacher. Miss Pepper would pick him up at the house in her small bus. She would play music and sing all the way to school, then she would park the bus and go into school with him, as she was also his personal aide. He loved her, and he loved going to school. They took many field trips together to apple orchards and to petting zoos. On one trip to a petting zoo, with his other aide, Miss Heather, we got a photo of him gagging while trying to pet one of the animals.

We were blessed to have a wonderful speech therapist who came to the house in the evenings, Miss Katherine. She taught him basic sign language and was able to get him to nod yes and no.

Because of his delays, he went to half-day kindergarten at five years old and didn't start full-day kindergarten till six years old at Mascoutah Elementary School. At recess, he had no friends to play with but loved to swing. The problem was that everyone else liked to swing too. If he didn't get a swing, he would cry until his turn, then cry again when his turn was over.

Devin's diet was very limited and unhealthy. He preferred anything with cheese! Scrambled eggs with cheese, grilled cheese, cheeseburgers (especially from McDonald's), and cheese pizza were the staples. If we wanted him to eat chicken, or fish, or even a baked potato, we would melt cheese on it. He was also a big fan of soda, especially Coca-Cola. Over the years he would cycle to Pepsi, Mountain Dew or others.

Donna packed his lunch every day because the school would almost never have anything he liked. She had to pack double chips and double desserts because he was always worried he might be hungry later in the day.

Most days he would bring things back home, but rarely did a second dessert survive the day.

Donna grew up in Mascoutah, and was always fond of a neighborhood called Coachlight, over by the city park. A much newer, much nicer brick home was available and we could afford it, so we moved across town.

During the time Devin was non-verbal, he developed a fondness for video games on the computer. He became so good at these games that eventually he would have to allow others to win at Quake, WWE or Mortal Kombat, or no one would want to play with him. He also became a movie fan. He couldn't handle the noise in the theatre, so had to watch at home. He had his favorites, like "Aristocats" and "The Indian in the Cupboard." He figured out how to get the VCR to auto-loop the parts he liked, so he could watch them over and over. Where there were scary scenes, he would run around a corner and hide as the scene passed, then walk back to his spot in front of the TV. You could see his spot as his feet had made indentions in the carpet and pad.

He loved movies so much that he would carry VHS boxes around with him, in the house, in the car, pretty much everywhere. He would cycle through the various movies, but typically grouped them by studio, like MGM or Disney.

By about age four, and with intensive speech- and music-therapy, Devin began to talk, and was able to become completely verbal over the next three to four years. He had also learned better eye contact and began to hold conversations, but really, was just answering questions, in more of an interview type of dialogue. As his communication improved, his crying diminished, which was wonderful.

Devin liked to jump on the trampoline, but his overall favorite outdoor activity was swinging. He was also a big fan of shooting baskets. Over the years, he would become very hard to beat at a game of HORSE.

I mentioned earlier that he had some tactile issues, or sensitivity to textures. Things like shaving cream and finger paint, when put in his hand, would make him gag. He loved the rubber bouncy floor in the McDonald's play place area, so much so that we had to watch, or he would lay down and lick it. Mr. Simon's team was able to figure out that while wearing rubber gloves, Devin could finger paint without gagging. He was so sensitive to tactile issues that there could be no tags or itchy sewn-on items or patterns on his clothing.

Devin took longer than typical to potty-train. He was almost eight years old before he was completely out of Pull-Ups. Anxiety was a driver in this. He was afraid of being laughed at or punished for wetting himself, even though he was never punished for such things. He was just so good-natured, that he never wanted to disappoint us. Even once fully able to go without the Pull-Ups, he didn't have the dexterity to manipulate zippers or snaps, so we had to get him elastic-waisted pants from Husky Fashions online.

Devin got along with all of Dave and Kelly's kids, but was closest to their youngest, Joe. They would spend time together playing wrestling or other video games whenever the families would get together.

Devin was extremely sensitive to fragrances. If we would use them in our house, he would break out head to toe in eczema. Even normal laundry detergents would cause him to breakout. Once we forgot this and used regular detergent. A couple days later he took off his T-shirt and looked like he had been painted red.

We are big believers in family vacations, where we are all away from our daily world, enjoying ourselves and each other, developing memories that would always be there regardless what else happens in life. We are so glad now that we took these trips and took so many pictures. Devin got to fly for the first time when we went to Wisconsin Dells. We could easily have driven there, but he was excited about the idea of flying. The trip was fantastic, except the one fully enclosed family water slide. All four of us jumped in. As we launched, our tube spun around and Devin ended up going backwards…in the dark! He was four kinds of fired up when we got off that ride, stomping around, mad, and talking to himself.

We also took a bigger trip, spending a week in Monterrey, Mexico. I chose Monterrey because I wanted the kids to get a feel for the difference between a Mexican and a U.S. city. They experienced firsthand the poverty, with young children at stoplights begging for money on the weekends. Devin loved the flights and enjoyed the different language, like when we ordered his hamburguesa con queso double from the drive-through at McDonald's or when we watched "The Hulk" in Spanish with English subtitles. He also enjoyed the amusement park, Plaza Sesamo. He was afraid of the log flume and the roller coaster but found some things he really liked. He enjoyed climbing the Cola de Caballo waterfall south of town, and driving up to Parque Ecologico Chipinque, about 7,300 feet up the mountain, with a scenic outlook over the city. We stayed at the Crowne Plaza hotel right downtown. We had a lot of funny things happen while there, like when Donna let go of the door to the tennis court and the door shattered, or when Kullen was tearing away with his teeth on a piece of bread from the buffet, only to have one of the restaurant workers come up and say, "Oh, no, sir, that is a decoration." Devin laughed so hard he about fell out of his chair, arms flailing and legs kicking. He liked the evenings in the hotel lobby with the bands playing local music.

Devin loved to camp. I should clarify – not in a tent. We tried to tent camp during his non-verbal years, at Dam West Campground, on Carlyle Lake, and it was miserable, he was pacing around inside the tent crying most of the time. We bought an old 19-foot Shasta camper from our friends, the Kecks, and he was all about it. He enjoyed sitting around the campfire having s'mores, walking the trails, swimming at the pool. Our second camper was a little bigger, and offered us the ability to have family movie time or game playing time in the camper each night. This quickly became his favorite part about camping. The simple things in life were the things he loved the most. Things like watching movies, playing board games, swinging together and taking walks. This is a key lesson we have learned and hope others can learn from Devin – time together, just enjoying each other's company, is what life is all about.

Devin and Kullen playing a game in the camper

Somewhere around six years old, Devin started developing bald spots on his head. We took him into Children's Hospital, and they determined it was Alopecia Areata. It was nothing to be concerned about in and of itself, but it is a side effect of long-term steroid use. They prescribed us a Rogaine foam to apply daily, but it was ineffective. This was just another headwind he would face in life. Not only was he the kid in class that made strange noises, but he was overweight from the steroids with patchy-balding hair and glasses. Somehow, though, he was always smiling.

Devin had unique joint flexibility. In some ways more flexible than typical, and in other ways the opposite. Let me explain. I played recreational soccer growing up, and one of the stretches we would do in warm-ups was called the Buddha stretch. To perform this, you sit on the ground with your back upright and your legs bent in a way that the soles of your feet touch each other. You bounce your legs a bit to loosen your hips, then grab your toes with your hands, and try to put your nose down to your toes. I've been doing this stretch daily for about 40 years now, and have never gotten closer than about six inches from my toes. Devin, on his first try, was able to put his nose flat-down on his toes without any effort at all. His hips were so flexible that he could sit Indian-style on the floor, but actually different than you and me. In normal Indian-style, your ankles cross. In Devin's style, one ankle actually crosses over the other thigh. His back would be perfectly straight, and he was completely comfortable. His hip flexibility was incredible. Beyond that, though, he was very stiff. For example, he could not get anywhere near his toes when doing toe-touches, and when he walked or ran, his knees and elbows seemed rigid.

Once Devin was fully able to speak, he began to order his own food at McDonald's. He loved their double cheeseburgers. He would order them specifically with pickles on them. As soon as we would sit down to eat, he would take the buns off, then the pickles off, then start scraping the cheese off with his fingers and eat all of that first, then the burgers. He would not eat the pickles or buns. Later in life, he would eat the burger on the bun but never grew to like the pickles so would order them without.

At a very young age, he became fond of researching things on the computer. He would spend hours understanding the differences in the types of sodas Coca-Cola offered or all the movies a particular studio had produced.

Devin loved the Mascoutah park. We lived a block from it, so he and I would walk over there so he could play in the playground or ride the swings. They had this ladder you could climb, then you ended up inside what looked like a big hamburger. I would hide below then poke my head out in different places, and he would laugh hysterically. He also really liked the public pool. As a family, we spent hundreds of hours there, swimming, playing catch, and enjoying snacks from the snack bar. To teach Devin to catch, we had to start by teaching him that squish balls don't hurt, so Kullen and I would let Devin throw them at us as hard as he could and we would let them hit us and we would make noises and fall over in the pool. Once he was not afraid to get hit, we spent time working on catching. He was a natural.

Donna ran a daycare in our house in Illinois, too, which afforded Devin several good friends. He also got to spend lots of time with his cousins, Kyle and Lindsey.

They were together with Devin every day after school, and all day, when schools were closed. They would jump on the trampoline, shoot hoops, watch movies and play games together.

Devin and Kullen with their cousins in our house on Coachlight.
Left to right, Devin, Kyle, William, Kullen, Lindsey, Zach

He tried to learn to ride a bike, and was plenty strong to do the pedalling, but could never get the balance of it. We tried multiple different training-wheel combinations, but they would just bend and he'd fall over. I ended up adding an attachment to my bike that hung a wheel and pedals off my seat-post. He was my tag-along buddy from that point forward. We rode around, mostly at campgrounds together.

We were quite active in the Mascoutah First Baptist Church. They had a Wednesday night program for kids, called Team Kid. Donna ran the inside, classroom and snack portion, and I ran the outside, energy-burning portion. We did this for several years. Devin really struggled with faith. Not so much the believing in Jesus part of it but the part that sin causes you to go to hell. He would stress over going to hell any time he had a bad thought. We tried to explain that once you are saved, God forgives you of those sins, and that's why Jesus was here. He never could come to grips with that part of it.

In 2003, when Devin was eight years old, we moved to Smyrna, Tennessee, about 20 miles southeast of Nashville, so I could take a plant manager opportunity at a greenfield startup with Tower Automotive, as a supplier to Nissan. We really liked the area because of all the hills and lakes, and the proximity to the city for things like Nashville Predators hockey games. We bought a split-level brick home on a hill, with basement garage. Devin's bedroom was on the top floor, as was Kullen's. Devin liked all the cool roof-angles and how they cut across with unique shapes in his room. Along with the garage, the basement had a family room, which we filled with a pool table, and a smaller room we setup as our theatre space. We got four connecting recliners and set them up facing our big screen TV. We grew into a pattern of Fridays being our pizza/movie nights. Sometimes we would go out for one or both, but most of the time, we were in our basement, with delivered pizza and some rented movies. This was good quality time, as the four of us – well, five, if you count Bobby, our Shi Tzu – each grabbed our

Snuggies, and spent a few hours together eating pizza, popcorn and candy, and talking about our week.

Devin fit right in at Rock Springs Elementary School. They had a buddy program, and his buddy was Alex. Alex was to help Devin around the school for his first week. In the middle of that week, while outside in our driveway shooting baskets, Devin spotted Alex two doors down. Alex happens to have a brother with special needs, so he was a natural friend for Devin. We have fond memories of Devin and Alex in their ninja costumes in the driveway, in the house playing video games, and even just sitting together taking turns completing a crossword puzzle. Outside the family, Alex was the one true friend Devin had in his life. There were others who came and went in short spurts, but only Alex was always there for him.

Devin bowling with Alex in Smyrna

Devin and Alex in our kitchen in Smyrna

Donna became friends with some other moms in the drop-off/pickup lanes at the school, and this led to Devin having some other friends, Ryan and Ian. Whenever we would get the families together, Devin would spend time with these guys, and he got along well with them, but he never was quite as close with them as he was with Alex.

The doctors at Vanderbilt Children's Hospital didn't believe the low-dose, every-other-day steroid helped, and recommended we take him off. We did, and the symptoms came back. We had to go back through the whole battery of tests, only to ultimately end up hitting him with another high dose of steroid, then backing it down. At this point we decided that no matter where we lived, we would commute back to St Louis annually so Dr. Shenoy could be his physician, and help to manage his ALPS. Unfortunately, this second round of intense steroid changed his body structure, and he would never again return to his naturally very lean build.

In the kitchen in Smyrna, we marked the heights of Kullen and Devin every few months, so they could see how much they were growing. We lived there about seven years, and over those years, Devin grew taller than his mom, and was super excited when it showed that way in the marks on the kitchen wall.

Between the ages of about nine and ten, he developed his own catch phrase that became a common phrase for the family. It started out that as bed time would draw near, he would ask if he could have one more Coke. Of course, the answer was no. Then he would say, how about a sip, or a drip or even a lick of Coke? We would convince him to wait till morning. Each day, as we'd go through this ritual, he would shorten it to where it became, not even a sipadripalickacokie?

Devin also really enjoyed Nashville Shores, a water park on the lake's west end. He was not much for the slides that didn't allow you to ride on a tube, as he didn't like the feel of the slide transitions on his back. If the slide allowed a tube, he was all about it. I remember one time when we were all there, and Devin felt stronger than Kullen for a minute, because Kullen had developed a fear of heights, and couldn't overcome the outdoor stairs to one of the slides.

We would travel back to Illinois to visit family five or six times a year, with our longest stays being around the Christmas holidays. We always stayed at his Grandma Jan's in Mascoutah. He enjoyed the road trips, but not so much the constant time with family. Often times, you would find him upstairs with me, laying on our backs across the bed, just talking, giving him a chance to de-stress. I remember teaching him how to throw a football, and get a good spiral. One time in Grandma Jan's driveway, we were able to throw and catch it 435 times without dropping it. He was jumping around and laughing the whole time.

Devin on the computer at Grandma Judy's

During one of these trips, on our return trip to Smyrna, Donna turned on some country music. This was the first choice of no one but her in the vehicle. I leaned over and whispered to Devin, that for the next few minutes, every time there was a pause of any kind in the song, he should say "I reckon," and see how long it took her to catch on. It was about five minutes later when she said "hey." Devin thought this was hilarious.

We took some other family vacations in this age-range, to places like Memphis and Gatlinburg. Every couple of years we would visit Donna's lifelong friend Melissa and her husband Sean, sometimes staying at a hotel near them, other times staying with them on their houseboat. A couple of times, we rode their ski boat over to the water park on the lake, and rode slides. In 2004, we took a family vacation in the Smoky Mountains. We rented a cabin in Sevierville with our friends Lou and Shannon, and their kids. We toured the state parks and Cade's cove, and just took in all the beauty in the area.

One weekend, it was girls' night, and Donna went out for dinner and drinks with some friends. The guys came over and brought the kids to our place to hang out. While playing hide and seek, Devin got onto a top bunk upstairs. He leaned over to see if anyone was in the room and got smacked right in the forehead by the ceiling fan. It sounded like a British police siren, as he screamed. It took a while for the bleeding to stop, and he was left with a divot. He carried that mark for the rest of his life.

In 2005, when Devin was ten years old, we visited Disney World. We stayed on property in the All Star

Sports Resort. There was a pool right outside our door, and we spent a lot of time there swimming and playing catch in the water. He enjoyed the theme parks, but at this age, was afraid of most rides, even the Goofy Barnstormer roller-coaster. We rode the basic ones and had a good time with the shows. One of the days we took a break from Disney and went out to Clearwater, on the Gulf Coast, near Tampa, and met some friends the Gass family, who were vacationing there at the same time. We spent a few hours on a pirate cruise, and had fish tacos on the beach. It was a nice, relaxing day. We spent a few more days at Disney, then on the way back, we stopped in Georgia and stayed on the houseboat with Melissa and Sean. Devin got to ride with me on a Sea-Doo for the first time and enjoyed it. One evening there was a water-balloon fight between our houseboat and the one tied-off next to us. Devin was all about it. You could hear the "eeee" sounds loud and clear. The water was pretty deep at the back of the boats, and so people were taking turns jumping off the back. Devin decided to try it. When he went, he just stepped off and didn't jump, and so if I didn't push him, he would hit the ski boat tied off below, so I pushed him. Unfortunately, this caused him to belly-flop. He had a life jacket on, but it was still uncomfortable. He came up all kinds of mad, yelling at me, until I explained why I did it.

Devin and Kullen with Woody at Disney World, 2005

Donna and I both grew up in small rural towns in Illinois. In the area, every small town would have a homecoming. This is a weekend picnic with fried food, carnival rides, tractor pulls, craft fairs and live music. Mascoutah always held theirs the first weekend in August, and Freeburg, where I grew up, the third weekend. We went to these every year; even after moving to Tennessee, we would hit them on alternating years. Devin loved the kids' swings, and rode them every year. One time he got sick on a barrel-spin ride and had to lay down for a while. I would ride the Ferris wheel with him every time. If he had friends or if Uncle Jeff or Aunt Debbie was nearby, he could ride some of the other, scarier rides.

He had absolutely no fear of carnival rides. Even the Hammerhead, which flips you over and over then turns and does it backwards, was no match for him.

Devin at the Mascoutah Homecoming
Left to right, William, Devin, Andrea, Zach, Bill, Donna

Devin had come such a long way in these early years, overcoming many obstacles, and developing his own unique, wonderful personality, and outlook on life. Considering the early prognosis of not even knowing if he would ever speak, we were thrilled with his progress. He still needed an IEP to ensure he got the minor workload modifications, therapies, and assistance he needed, but he was handling "normal" life.

For any parents out there who have recently received the horrible diagnosis of autism, this is just one example, and the outcome is truly different for everyone, but I encourage you to do what Donna did, and spend serious time with the school faculty and push for every possible form of therapy, assistance and workload modification you can get. Research, ask other parents what they do, and force your local school to hire people if needed, or pay your out of district rates to take your child where they can get everything. There is no way to know which things will break them through, so try them all.

Chapter 2

THE MIDDLE YEARS

———

Devin was a people-pleaser. He never wanted to get in trouble and always wanted others to be proud of him. He was also black-and-white or letter-of-the-law in his approach. If he was ever told not to do something, he would never do it. I can't recall a single time in his life where he ever lied to anyone, talked about anyone, cheated, stole, or did anything that would have given anyone the chance to be disappointed in him. If he got into a situation that stressed him out, instead of arguing or fighting, he would walk away, pace around, make his "eeee" sound, and talk to himself. You could tell by the pitch if he was happy or frustrated, higher pitch was happy, lower pitch was frustrated.

After three years in Smyrna, Devin transitioned to Rock Springs Middle school. This school was a culture shock, as they were almost militant in their approach to discipline, punishing kids for walking out of line, talking in the hall, dying their hair a non-natural color or more than one color, not tucking in their shirts, and the like. Quickly, his anxiety grew to the point he developed full OCD. It was heartbreaking to hear him upstairs at night, walking from his room to the restroom, flushing the toilet and washing his hands, going back to his room, then heading back to the restroom, exactly 12 times before he could lay down and allow himself to sleep. This was just one example of many, including cycling locks multiple times, and other common OCD characteristics. It took years of therapy to help him overcome this.

One key lesson we learned from this phase of his life is that we should have been as focused on the culture of the school, as we were on his IEP for things like workload modifications and therapies. As parents, we were the only ones who could advocate for his needs, and we missed this part somehow. While we were eventually able to work him through it, it caused unnecessary hardship throughout the remainder of his life.

Devin's first encounter with bullying came during his time in middle school. Some kids in the lunchroom convinced him to smash ketchup packets. When he smashed them, the kids would all laugh, and so he thought they really liked it, so he kept on doing it. When he got caught, they all left. He was called to the office to be disciplined, which was devastating for him. The school offered to paddle him if we'd like, which we, of course, declined. For him, all it took was to be in trouble, and to talk through it with us, no other punishment was necessary.

Devin also developed clinical depression because he was on the higher end of the autism spectrum in terms of functionality and realized he was different, and with only one true friend outside the family, and outside Kullen's group of friends who always liked him, found himself alone with his thoughts on a regular basis. Donna and I would spend as much time with him as he would allow, playing games, watching movies or riding around, but it's not the same as having friends to hang out with. He would be found swinging or pacing around the yard or sitting/bouncing on the trampoline with his iPod and earbuds, off in his own world. The iPod was never in his pocket, because he would continually click the volume up and down the entire time he was listening.

We got our first boat, a runabout, in spring 2007, and Devin loved it. We hauled it around to a few lakes, but found we preferred J Percy Priest Lake, the one closest to us, the best. We kept the boat on a lift at Four Corners Marina in Lavergne, Tennessee. The boat bounced over the waves, and Devin would ride up front and raise his arms, as if on a ride at an amusement park. His favorite towable tube was shaped like a wave-runner. He could sit up and hold the handles. He also enjoyed the Big Mable tube, shaped like a couch that he and Alex, or he and Ryan could ride together. Devin used to get a good laugh when people would fail at their first wakeboarding or kneeboarding attempt, or get thrown wildly off a tube, like the time Kullen and Lindsey did complete backflips at the same time off the Big Mable. Devin was first to the door every time I asked who wanted to go boating, especially if we planned to stop at the marina restaurant afterward for fried green beans. Alex spent lots of time out on the water with Devin, and he could not have been happier.

Dave and Kelly came down and spent some weekends with us and brought their kids. Devin had a ball hanging out with them on the water and at the house. My cousin Mike and his wife JoAnn stopped by with their kids and spent a day on the water with us, on one of their vacations, too. These were great times.

My brother, Jeff, would come down and stay with us several times a year, usually around Super Bowl, and the summer holidays. We would spend lots of time as a group boating, bowling, playing games and watching movies. I remember one night we had grilled and Jeff had just sat down in the recliner with his plate of food, when Devin, without looking, did his normal nightly toss of dirty laundry from the catwalk between the upstairs bedrooms, and it landed directly on Jeff's plate, knocking it out of his hands and all over the floor. Jeff freaked out and Devin was terrified. By morning, though, it became a pretty funny memory for all of us.

We took another big family vacation in 2007. We went to Cancun, Mexico, and stayed at the Moon Palace resort. As expected, Devin loved the flights. The resort was great. We shared a big family-style hotel room, and the housekeepers made different animal shapes out of the towels by the hot tub each day. Devin loved that the fridge was stocked with all the soda he could drink and that 24-

hour pizza room-service was included. One day we went to Chichen Itza, the Mayan pyramids. The scenery was great. The fire ants that attacked his brother, Kullen, were not so great. Another day, we ventured out and took a taxi to Señor Frog's downtown. The taxi was the scariest ride of our lives, as the driver held his cell phone to his ear while driving a stick shift in traffic. We did get him to stop along the way and got a nice picture of the four of us with a great water view as a background. A different day, we took a boat ride to a water park, and Devin had a blast. One day, he and I jumped in a kayak and headed out into the waves. It was hard to go far, but he thought it was cool. The best part of the whole trip was that Devin got to parasail for the first time. I rode with him. I'm terrified of heights, but wanted him to enjoy himself. Donna and Kullen rode out on the boat but didn't want to try it. It turned out to be a wonderful experience. The hum of the boat some 500 feet below, looking as small as a kid's toy, the smell of the ocean, the sun, the gentle breeze, and… absolute peace and quiet, just me and one of my favorite people in the whole world, was priceless. The water was crystal clear, we could see the bottom, as if it were only a couple feet deep. Devin was smiling, as big as I'd ever seen. This turned out to be one of the best days of his life. I'm so glad we did it. He loved it so much that the following summer he asked if we could do it again. The closest place we could find was Tan Tar A resort in Lake of the Ozarks. We went and Devin got to parasail again. Donna and Kullen actually tried it too.

Dinner in the Moon Palace Resort
Cancun, 2007

Me and Devin Parasailing
Cancun, 2007

Photo the cab driver took on our way to Señor Frogs

I mentioned how autism typically puts kids outside the circle, watching others enjoy things. Devin was no different. He would watch us as we watched movies, to see how we would react to the funny parts. Sometimes he'd see the movies in advance so he'd know when funny parts were coming and could watch our reactions. When asked about it later; he would say that he knew the appropriate emotions, and would laugh but wouldn't always really feel it. He said the same was the case with grief or sadness – he knew it was appropriate but didn't always feel it.

One evening, Kullen, Devin and Alex were on the catwalk, kicking a home-made stuffed crochet soccer ball back and forth. All was going well, till Devin tried to really boot one. He misfired, and drove his foot into the floor, popping the nail on his big toe out, from the base.

It was a bloody mess, and all three were yelling until we came to the rescue and bandaged him up.

For one of Devin's birthday parties, we decided to rent an inflatable bouncy house, and set it up in the driveway. As luck would have it, we had a near-record heat wave, so it was like 100 degrees in May. We spent most of the day in the garage, with the AC vents open, and fans blowing. We were all a sweaty mess, but Devin was still smiling, as big as ever. His friends Alex, Judah and Ryan were there along with Kullen and his friends Kyle and Hunter.

Devin loved adventure. He would go with me any time anywhere. He loved to travel, loved boy's nights, movie nights, bowling, anything to get out and go for a ride, and have some food and/or some fun. One time we took the camper, just the two of us to a campground in Lebanon, Tennessee, just to get away for a couple days.

Devin's anxiety continued to worsen. Things he used to really enjoy became stressful, for example, boating would mean he would need to wear sunscreen, and he would not be comfortable sleeping after if he didn't take another shower, so he decided he'd rather not go boating. After a few years of counselling, and with some medications, we were able to get him through this phase of life, but I can't overstate how devastating it was. This psychological condition kept him away from doing things he loved.

Devin was a grammar junkie. Everything he did was in perfect grammar. Even when he would send someone a text from his phone, it would include proper punctuation and capitalization. Once, he sent a text to Lindsey, and wrote "for this next text, I'm going to use text slang" and then included his text to her. One time he was on YouTube correcting grammar and ran into another bully, who cursed at him for doing such a thing on a site like YouTube. He was distraught, and Donna spent a while with him, explaining how some people are just hurtful by nature, especially online, where they don't have to confront the person they are bullying.

Devin was not picky about music, but was always drawn to rap, listening to stars like Eminem and LL Cool J. The primary draw was the word play. He wanted to be a star, just like them. He was always online researching them, the disagreements they had that inspired their songs, and so on. You could ask him a question about any song or artist in the genre and he could tell you a story. It always started with "Well, you see…" I really miss these stories.

His love for word-play carried over into poetry. This gave him the ability to dabble with word-play of his own, and he also loved the structure of the various poems, where the number of syllables in each line determined the type of poem. The poems on the following pages were written for a middle school poetry project. For all the struggles Devin had with fitting into middle school, this project sparked a life-long interest.

Haiku

Glistening Sunshine
Shining on the pretty lake
Makes me want to swim

Name Poem

Determined to be strong
Energetic
Very hard worker
Interested in lots of things
Never mean

Wonderful
Intelligent
Not disrespectful
Trustworthy always
Extra nice friend
Really faithful

A-B-C Poem

Days are long
Ending never
Finally it's time
Going home
Yes! We made it!

I Remember
Parallel Poetry

I remember being small
I remember wishing to grow
I remember the marks on the wall
I remember standing on tiptoe
I remember when my legs weren't long
I remember eating food to grow
I remember wanting to be strong
I remember growing but I don't know
I remember wondering when I grew
I remember being as tall as you

Will I be happy?
Question Poem

Will I be happy?
Am I going to be successful?
Will I find a great life?
Will I be happy?
What job will I have?
Will I be proud of me?
Will I be happy?
Have I made the right choices?
How can I be sure?
Will I be happy?
Will I have many friends?
Will I be smiling?
Will I be happy?

Goo Goo Cluster

Since 1912
First combo candy bar,
Delicious, unique, round
Tradition!
Simpler, slower paced time
Enjoy at Cracker Barrel

Diamante

Weekends
Fast, fun
Sleeping, Playing, Eating
Freedom, Movies, Lessons, Teachers
Listening, Learning Studying
Long, Hard
Weekdays

Limericks

There once was a school called Rock Springs
Where kids could learn all kinds of things
Students came in each day
And then went on their way
With a ton of new knowledge to bring

I Flew Very High

I was so scared to give it a try
I never thought that I could fly
But in the seat with my seat belt snapped

They lifted me high and the parachute flapped
The wind took us up, just me and my dad
And I flew like a bird and boy was I glad
I am so happy I made myself try
Because I'll never forget when I flew very high

Find Your Place
A Sonnet

Life can be a scary ride
Until you find your place
Sometimes you want to run and hide
So no one sees your face
I look around but all I see
Are not so friendly eyes
But when I look up past the trees
I see the bright blue skies
The sunshine lighting up the day
Can make me feel much better
But when the clouds get in the way
The rain makes me feel wetter
So everyday I try to face
Each problem the best I can
So when I finally find my place
I can be a real great man

I am Devin
Free-Verse Poem

I really hope for success
So I'm prepared for work
I fear the occurrence of my future
Because thoughts and feelings change
I love to watch motion pictures
They basically capture my interest
I also enjoy surfing the internet
It is very thrilling to do research
Not on anything specific though
Just anything I find interesting
I am a smart boy named Devin
And these are things about me

Chapter 3

THE LATER YEARS

———

For many years, we hosted New Years' Eve parties, regardless of where we were living. One year in Tennessee, we had a huge gathering, about 30 people, and everyone was playing Wii Boogie, where you sing and dance along with the video game. Devin was all about it, but as we watch videos of the event, he was most excited watching others embarrass themselves. He was jumping up and down in his camo pants, squealing loudly with his arms punching upward. He had the biggest smile that night. We also played Wii Bowling. Devin had practiced and that night bowled a perfect 300 game! He had a unique style. He would stand very close to the TV, like within 12 inches. He would swing his arm down, then as he swung up to horizontal, he would jump and twist his whole body 90 degrees to the left at the same time, so he ended up with his right shoulder facing the TV. I have no idea how it worked, but he was able to bowl a perfect 300 game a couple of more times doing it this way.

Donna worked at a small bank in Smyrna and became friends with many of her co-workers. Several of them would bring their families over for New Year's Eve and other gatherings. Her boss at the time, Anne became a great friend for Devin. They would sit and watch movies together, play Wii, or just hang out. She has remained a friend of the family through the years.

Devin and Anne in Smyrna

In 2009, we took a family vacation to the Smoky Mountains. This time just the four of us. We stayed at a resort there that had an indoor water park. We spent a lot of time in their wave pool. We hit the touristy things, like Ripley's Believe it or Not, Dollywood, and indoor skydiving. I couldn't talk Devin into trying that, but Kullen and I did it, and Devin enjoyed watching us fall.

Devin and Kullen in the Smokies 2009

Devin and Donna 2009

Devin and me 2009

Devin with me and Kullen and Four Corners Marina 2009

Later in 2009 I was working for Visteon Corporation at the time of the big recession, when the government was bailing out the big three automotive companies. Chrysler filed bankruptcy. Visteon followed suit not long-after, and I was in a position to sell or close all the plants I was responsible for. Visteon had two opportunities for me. One was to move to Buenos Aires and become country manager running three operations. The other was to remain in Smyrna but be responsible for the quality of plants in India, Mexico and the Czech Republic – which would mean brutal travel. I was looking around for work in the Smyrna area but had not reached out for recruiter assistance. Devin, in his straight, direct, honest way said, "Why don't we sell everything and live in the camper, so we don't have to move?" Our logical minds kicked in, and we brushed this off – to this day, we have some level of regret that we didn't take his lead – obviously we couldn't do exactly what he asked, but staying put could have been a good thing.

Donna's mom, Jan, had survived breast cancer but continued to struggle with diabetes. She had fallen a couple times because she forgot to check her sugar before giving herself insulin. I reached out to a friend/former business associate, to see if his company had any needs, and the timing was perfect, so I began working for Fall Protection Systems in St Louis, and we moved back closer to family, to Highland, Illinois, in June 2010, so we could take care of her. Joe, Dave and Kelly's youngest, came and spent a few days us, which helped Devin with the transition.

Devin at Joe's house

On July 27, 2010, just six weeks after moving to Highland, Devin found blood spots or bruises all over his body, even places like his tongue and eyelids. We took him to Children's Hospital, where they diagnosed the issue as Idiopathic Thrombocytopenia Purpura (ITP) – a drop in platelets, with no known cause, accompanied by bruising or the blood spots we saw, called petechia, pronounced puh-tee-kee-uh. A full description of ITP can be found on the Johns Hopkins website[(F)]. As I searched for an easy way to describe this disorder, I came across one at HealthLine that was well done: "In ITP, the immune system produces antibodies against platelets. These platelets are marked for destruction and removal by the spleen, which lowers the platelet count. The immune system also appears to interfere with cells responsible for normal platelet production, which can further lower the number of platelets in the blood stream."[G]. As more has been learned about this disorder, the "I" has begun to change from idiopathic, to immune. The strange thing about this ITP is that he never had it before we moved to Highland. He was treated with one dose of Winrho (Itraveneus Immunoglobulin, or IVIG) and his platelets were monitored closely. IVIG has been around a long time, but has only been tested in ITP in since the early 1980s, becoming well-established in the mid 1990s[H]. Our insurance at the time of Devin's first bout still considered IVIG experimental at the time it was needed. Over a few weeks' time, Devin's platelets climbed to within the normal range, and all was good. Looking back through medical records we see a note in September of 2010 where the doctor had concerns about amitriptyline possibly causing the ITP, and that we agreed to ween him off that medication.

On May 25, 2011, less than a year after Devin's bout with ITP, Donna also got ITP, and she, too, never had it before moving there. This led us to believe that it has to be triggered by something environmental. The doctors unanimously shot down this concept, saying it's triggered by coming in contact with a virus, and the immune system overreacting and killing off platelets. But as you research the disorder, you will find that it's common in chemotherapy and other treatments, which is the body reacting to a chemical, so we continued to ask, why couldn't other chemicals cause it? Our house happened to be in a neighborhood of converted farmland, with cornfields on three sides, within about a quarter mile in any direction, where chemicals were used for fertilizing, insect and weed controls. Donna's bout was treated with high dose prednisone, and she recovered fine.

One thing great about Highland was the friendships we developed with the neighbors. The majority of them are all related, and they pulled us into the family. Shirley (Mema) was next door, and her daughter Kelly was across the street with her husband Gary and their kids. Mema's other daughters, Sharon and her husband Rob, and Lori and her husband Garon, moved into the neighborhood over the years. They are all fantastic people. We are closest with Gary and Kelly, as we met them first, in fact before we even moved in, I was working in the yard, and they rode over on their golf cart to say hi. Over the years, we spent many evenings together around bonfires, swimming, playing volleyball, watching football or playing board games. Every couple of months, we would rotate locations and get together, each bringing a dish from a certain nationality like "this month is Italian night" and share dinner together. Some of our best dinners were when Gary made his famous chili or chicken and dumplings. But life was not always rosy, and we have all been there for each other during some very difficult times medically. We went to their kids' birthday parties, and they did the same for ours. One year, when Devin was about 18, Gary got him a Barbie doll as a gift. The video clip of him opening it is hysterical. He loved it!

Devin and Kullen playing Go Fish Yourself

As Devin got a bit older, we had to hide the clippers, or sometimes, if he was too warm, he would completely clip his head bald, like Pedro in Napoleon Dynamite. Sometimes he would even remove his eyebrows!

Devin encountered bullying again in high school, things like, "If you carry this box around for me, you can be in our club." So he carried the box around all day, until Donna spotted him and addressed it. Another time, a boy said, "If you wear this necklace for me, you can be my boyfriend," so Devin did it though he was unsure if he even wanted a boyfriend.

Devin tried variations of martial arts at different times. Back in Smyrna, as a family, we tried Tang Su Do, but that didn't last long. Devin decided to try karate in Highland. All was good except the amount of noise when the class would all yell at the same time, so we switched it to private lessons. He stuck it out for about a year, to the point he broke his first board, then got tired of it again.

In 2012, we took a big family vacation to France and Germany. As expected, Devin loved the flights. One day, I asked him what he loved so much about flying. He said, "I don't have to make any decisions, there is no stress." As I planned the trip, I wanted to ensure we had some time driving on the Audubon, so we rented a car. Our long flights were to and from Stutgart. We spent a few days in Paris, where we toured the Louvre and the Eifel Tower. We went up to the primary platform, and the view was great. Devin wanted to go to the top, but while he and I lined up, he was starting to stress out. I asked if he changed his mind, and he said yes, so we didn't go up. This is something else I regret, as I know he would have loved it once up there. We also spent a day at Euro Disney. There was a McDonald's a block from our hotel, so Devin was good to go. Kullen liked it, too, because they served Heineken, and he was old enough to drink there. After Paris, we stayed a night in Strasbourg and checked out the astronomical clock at the Notre Dame Cathedral. There were no American restaurants, so we went to a local place. Devin got to try head cheese for the first time. He thought it was good. We then took a ferry across Lake Konstanz on our way to Garmisch. We enjoyed the Alpine village feel there. Devin was glad to see they had a Pizza Hut. We spent the final few days in Munich, where we got to see the Rathaus Glockenspiel clock in Marienplatz, and have dinner at the original Hofbrauhaus.

Somewhere along the way in the mountains of southern Germany, our car overheated. This was an adventure all its own. I had picked up a burner phone when we first arrived, which came in handy at this point. We made our way to a gas station to let the car cool down. While waiting, we walked across the street to a small restaurant, where Devin got to enjoy ordering pizza from someone who did not speak English. After lunch, we found the nearest Hertz and traded vehicles, to a small stick shift station wagon. We were back in business. Kullen and Devin really enjoyed going more than 100 miles an hour and hearing the street names, like Flugenhafenstrasse, as they came across the GPS.

All of us at Disneyland Paris 2012

The three guys standing like a statue in France

Donna, Kullen and Devin outside castle Neuschwanstein Germany

All of us at Hofbrauhaus Munich

In 2013 we took a vacation to the Lake of the Ozarks, and rented a condo from some friends of ours, Rob and Sharon. We took our runabout with us. During the week, it was fun running from the condo, at about mile marker one up to the restaurant-bars along the water each mile, or so. We found a place to parasail at this end of the lake. This guy was sending people up, then on the way down, dipping their legs in the water, for a small fee, before lifting them again and bringing them in. Because of Devin's mosquito allergy, and the fact that he'd dug his legs up that week, and because of the bacteria in the lake, we declined the dip option. The guy decided to give us a freebee and dipped Devin anyway. The following week, we were in Anderson Hospital as Devin had a staph infection in his legs. It was at this point Devin decided he was pretty much done getting into any lake water.

All of us at a German restaurant, Lake of the Ozarks 2013

Later in 2013, a former colleague of mine reached out with a career opportunity I could not pass up. It allowed me to get back into a global company, with multiple-plant responsibility, with a significant pay increase, without having to move. The downside was that it would require about 60% travel. We decided to take the opportunity, and I joined Assa Abloy in January 2014.

Around this time, as Jan's condition was worsening, Mema would come spend lots of time with her, sitting and chatting, reading, or just being together. Jan loved those visits.

In May 2014, Devin graduated from Triad High School in Troy, Illinois. What an emotional time for us, given the start he had in life. To go from non-verbal to integrated classrooms with full-time aides and being removed from class for therapy and special classes, to graduating from a normal high school, normal classroom, with only an IEP for minor coursework modifications. He had overcome all the odds. It was incredible. Something else very cool about this graduation was that our good friend and neighbor, Kelly, was on the school board, and was the one who presented him his diploma.

Graduation 2014
Left to right, Kyle, Lindsey, Maddie, Devin, Brad, donna, Chad,
Brady, Trent, me, Jeff, Debbie, Kyle, Mark

Kelly and Devin

For our family vacation in 2014, we took a Caribbean cruise. We got to spend a day on the beach in Haiti, and climbed up a huge waterfall in Jamaica. Half-way up, Devin took the opt-out and waited for us at the top, where we found him being sold on a wood turtle with his name carved in its shell. The most fun for all of us was actually the time spent together on the ship. We went to every available show and activity. The ship was Royal Caribbean's Oasis of the Seas, their largest at the time. It was designed with a central park down the center and two sets of rooms running the length of the ship such that all rooms had balconies – some facing the water, some facing the park. On about the tenth floor, there was a zip line that ran diagonally about 100 feet from one side to the other. Devin asked me if I would ride it. I told him that if he did it, I would go. It took him about a minute to get both feet off the platform, but he was able to do it. Afterward, he felt such a huge sense of accomplishment. I stuck to my word and did it, too. It was horrifying, but I'm glad I did it. We all liked it so much we took another cruise a few years later.

Kullen Devin and Donna on our first cruise

Devin and Donna on our first cruise

Devin doing his Titanic pose on a glass floor about 13 stories above the ocean on our second cruise

All of us on formal night on our second cruise

In the airport headed for the second cruise

Devin started a job at a local grocery chain in the summer 2014, bagging groceries, and retrieving carts from the parking lot. He did well in this job for about a year. Donna was his primary driver, but he preferred when Mema would give him a ride, especially if it was nice out and they could take the Mustang. Eventually, Devin got a different supervisor who didn't really understand autism, and his need to pace around during gaps when there were no customers needing bagging, and she became strict, and gave him sub-par performance reviews. Often, Donna would open the door to his room, and he would be crying. We decided at that point to stop working there, and focus on taking some college classes part time.

While working at the grocery store, Devin became a member of the Illinois Center for Autism (ICA), which had a monthly event called Face to Face, where the workers would facilitate a night out for folks in their late teens with autism. They did lots of fun things, like bowling, movies, game nights, and visits to places like arcades. One time, they met at Centerfield in O'Fallon, Illinois. This is a cool place with mini golf, go-cart racing, bumper boats, batting cages, and an arcade. We got snacks and went alongside of the building to sit and eat. Devin sat first and happened to choose a plastic chair that had a bad leg, and when he sat, it broke, and he fell to the ground. I was behind him, so he jumped up yelling at me, saying "Why did you do that?" He thought I had kicked his chair out from under him. Once I showed him that it had broken, he calmed down and enjoyed his evening.

Jan lived in the bedroom next to Devin for three of the first four years we lived in Highland. She had again come into a bout with cancer, this time in the liver and pancreas. Devin would see her every day, and she would make a point to talk with him, even sometimes when he didn't really feel like talking. They were very close. In July 2014, she lost her battle with cancer. Donna and Devin were talking about it, and he said that with autism, "I can't truly feel what everyone else feels. Grandma Jan is gone, and that is sad, and I know I should be crying, but I never really cried about it."

Renth Family in Highland
Left to right. Back row, Mark, Debbie, Bill, Donna, me.
Middle row Lindsey, Irene, Jan, Kullen. Front row,
Kyle William, Devin, Zach

Devin with Great Grandma Irene

In late summer 2014, we were hit by a hail storm that destroyed all our roof and gutters and some siding. It also totalled our camper. We began to search for a camper, but at the same time, Jan's Hospice nurse told us about a subdivision on Carlyle Lake, that we had never heard of. We found an older mobile home with a lake view out the kitchen windows, an attached family room, detached garage, and boat dock, and decided to go that route instead of the camper route. The advantage was there would be no setup as compared to camping, this would always be ready when we got there. We began using this about once a month starting in the spring 2015, and Devin really enjoyed getting away for the weekends. The fact that we had Internet, McDonald's was within a couple miles, and Pizza Hut would deliver there, made it even better than camping. Devin also enjoyed the park at Dam West, where he could go for walks and listen to music, or spend some time on their swing sets.

Devin and Kullen were very close. While they would spend most of their days apart, there was always at least one hour each day that they were together watching a stand-up comedy, playing a video game, swimming, or just being brothers. Unfortunately, Devin got some bad news as Kullen made the decision in March 2015 to move back to Tennessee to live with his friend, Kyle. As is always the case, the intent was to stay in close contact and play together online after the move, but once he moved, it was hard to find time for that. Kullen came back to visit us a few times a year, and I took Devin down to visit him, and to see Anne a few times, too. We couldn't go to Smyrna without making a stop at Karin's Custard. He loved their caramel shakes.

We took a family vacation in June 2015 to Panama City, Florida. Kullen had just started a job in Tennessee, so couldn't join us, and while this felt strange at first, we made the most of it. We found something to do together each day up till about 1 p.m. – we parasailed, rode in a helicopter, and spent time at Pier Park riding their amusement rides, ate at Hofbrauhaus, and Dick's Last Resort, and went to see movies, then Donna and I would hit the beach in the afternoon while Devin caught up on some Internet time. Each evening, we'd get cleaned up and find dinner together, then play some games in the condo.

Devin parasailing in Panama City 2015

Me and Devin outside a restaurant in Panama City

Driving was a struggle for Devin. He had too much anxiety about what the drivers around him might do, what he would do if there was construction, or what others would think about him if he drove too slowly. We did have fun with the driving practice, though. I would drive over to the Highland Middle School parking lot in our Expedition, and let him take over. We would spend about 30 minutes taking laps, making figure-eights, and practicing parking. I would say, "Take this left, then park in the last space on the right." We'd get out and take a look, and if he was over the line a few feet, which happened most of the time, I'd say, "Whoops, you ran over grandma! Let's try again," and he would laugh, then hop in and try again. He was able to get up to about 35 miles per hour on backroads, but was never comfortable in traffic. For this reason, Donna drove him wherever he needed to go.

Devin liked being in Highland because he got to spend time with his uncle Jeff. They would play WWE on X Box One, and you could hear them laughing from the basement and all the way across the house. Jeff could hold his own, unlike the rest of us, so Devin really enjoyed playing with him. Jeff came over a lot, because he lived just a few minutes away, and we hung out, swam, watched movies, and played board games together.

I mentioned that Devin was always worried he would disappoint. Well, he was also afraid to confront anyone, because if they would come back at him, he would not know how to respond, and he was also not completely certain if a person was serious or joking. Over the years, Kullen would tease Devin, and because of this concern, Devin would typically walk away and mumble to himself. On one particular evening, after years of us encouraging him to stick up for himself, he actually responded calling Kullen a dick, and the whole room erupted. Even Kullen gave him a high five. Devin jumped up and down and squealed with relief that he had actually done it. While we don't condone name calling, we were certainly happy he stood up for himself.

There was a wooden swing set in the yard when we bought the house in Highland. Devin loved to swing. Unfortunately, one day he was out there swinging, and his swing fell off the set and he landed on his backside. He got up stomping mad. I went to the hardware store and got industrial strength parts to repair it. After a couple weeks he built confidence and began swinging again. About a year later, he was swinging and it broke again. This time he was marching all around the yard complaining about the unsatisfactory piece of equipment. Donna and I spent some time online and ended up ordering an adult swing set from Component Playgrounds, where each seat was rated to 500 pounds. Devin helped as I put a rope around the wooden set and used my truck to yank it over to the burn pile. He lit the fire for me, and smiled the whole time. Gary came over and helped us build the new swing set, and Devin never had another issue or concern about swinging.

Devin on the old wooden swing set in Highland

Devin also loved to pace around. It was not uncommon for him to walk laps around our two-acre yard. If the weather was bad, we'd find him in the detached garage, listening to music on his phone, and pacing around inside.

On one of our trips to Georgia, we spent some time in Chattanooga, on another trip we toured the World of Coca-Cola, and on another we went to a pay-per-view wrestling match. Devin loved it. Later in life, he would come to understand it was choreographed, something I regret telling him, but he still loved the hype, and the crazy things and special moves the wrestlers would do. On that same trip, we visited the water park with Melissa and Sean again, and Devin decided to try the zip line. He and I climbed up the hill, to what seemed like about 75 feet above the lake, and a zip line about a quarter-mile long. Since he had done it on the cruise, he had no fear at all. He took off down the hill, across a road, the water park, and the cove of the lake, to meet Donna on the other side. He loved it!

Devin and Kullen in Chattanooga 2006

WWE Match in Atlanta 2009

World of Coca Cola, Atlanta 2010

My mom always spent a lot of time trying to ensure the holidays were great. One year she got us all black tee-shirts, with a sign on the front reading "It's a Winter Thing, You Wouldn't Understand." Another year, instead of getting gifts for anyone, she planned a trip to Branson and gave that as a gift instead.

Christmas in Branson 2013 Left to right, Jerry, Judy, Jeff, Brad, me, Devin, Kullen, Brady, Trent, Donna, Maddie, Chad

Thanksgiving 2015 in Highland
Left to right, Kullen, Darren, Celine, Chad, me, Jerry, Josh, Judy,
Jeff, Brad, Devin, Donna

I mentioned that Devin never wanted to break a rule. This sometimes conflicted with his desperate desire to fit in. One time, he went to the movies with Kullen, Jake, Aaron, Abby and Sarah. The group chose an R-rated movie. Devin was so worried he would get in trouble, that he told the ticket agent they were all under 18. Everyone got upset with him, and he couldn't understand why. He thought he was keeping them all out of trouble.

Over the holidays at the end of 2015, we ran into an issue of meal moths in the house. We were dumbfounded as to the source. After much investigation, we found they came from an old box of breakfast cereal in the pantry. It had been in there a long time, and the bag inside was full of them. Terminix came to the house to spray inside the kitchen area, and to hang pheromone traps. They applied a couple treatments in January. They came back to spray for general insect treatment outside the house in March.

On March 23, 2016, Donna had another bout of ITP. Her platelets were over 300,000 on 3/9, but had fallen to 6,000 by 3/21. After CT scans, she was admitted for five consecutive days of IVIG with steroids, and a first dose of Rituxan, which at the time was part of the regimen in chemotherapy for the treatment of cancer.[1] I was surprised to see the hazard label on the bag when it was brought in, also when I heard all the warnings about her bodily fluids for 24 hours after the treatment. Ultimately, it took four weekly doses of Rituxun to get her platelets to remain at a relatively safe level, above 15,000. Looking back, we were thinking maybe the meal moth treatments had some correlation to the timing of ITP, but it doesn't appear so, as you can see from the ITP timeline in Appendix 3.

Life in Highland became more of a struggle when Donna's brother's family began to consume her life. All four in the family have mental conditions. As Jan was about to pass away, she asked Donna to look after them. At the time, we didn't realize the magnitude of that request. They are constantly in need of something, and Donna has a caring, loving heart, so she was completely absorbed. On the surface, Devin seemed okay with it whenever mom had to run to take care of them, but inside, he was becoming lonelier.

In fall 2016, we took a family vacation to Las Vegas and San Diego. The plan was to go in August, but Devin's cousin, Zach, was riding his bike and hit by a pickup truck, leaving him in a coma for many months, and eventually blind and in a wheelchair, so we delayed to October. Kullen was able to join us on this trip, so the gang was back together for another adventure. We started in Vegas. There, we took in the Beatles Love show at the Mirage, and a couple others. Devin, Donna and I rode the High Roller Ferris wheel. This one goes 550 feet up, and you are in a ball on the outside of the wheel. It moves so slowly that you can't tell it's moving until you get up close, and it doesn't stop for people to get on and off. You do that while it's moving. By the time we got about half way up, Donna and I were sitting down, backs against the wall, terrified. Devin was up doing the running man and other dances to the music they were playing. He had no fear and was completely happy. Unbeknownst to me, Devin had done some research about things to do in Vegas, and set me up for some craziness, as he talked me into taking him onto the roof of the Stratosphere space needle for some rides. He rode the Insanity, which is a mechanical arm that hangs out over the strip, about 1,100 feet in the air, then spins you as you tip out and face down. We rode the Big Shot together. They buckle you in, then launch you 180 feet straight up, then you drop and do it a few more times. As usual, I was terrified, but he got me to do it, and I'm so glad he did. We drove to San Diego. We hit Little Italy and the Gaslamp Quarter, went to the zoo, which was very nice, went to the beach for lobster tacos at

World Famous, and hiked in Torrey Pines. We toured the USS Midway aircraft carrier, and took a tour/cruise of the harbour. Looking back, we did the trip backwards. San Diego is wonderful, but after the thrills and excitement we had in Vegas, it was a bit ho-hum.

Devin and Kullen outside the Beatles Love Show, Las Vegas 2016

Devin on top of the Stratosphere Las Vegas, about to ride the Insanity

Devin and Donna about to get on the High Roller Las Vegas

All of us on a hike in Torrey Pines near San Diego

Later in fall 2016, the sadness became worse when Devin's Uncle Jeff decided to move to Florida to live with his girlfriend, Tracy, and her daughter, Sierra. As was the case when Kullen moved to Tennessee, there were good intentions of connecting regularly to play games online, but as we all know, life happens, and those game-playing times quickly faded away. Donna and I would spend every evening and most weekends watching movies and playing board games with Devin, but the distance to Alex, Kullen and Jeff left Devin devastatingly lonely.

Donna did some more research and found an organization called PTOEC, part of the Special Olympics program, and got Devin involved in their bowling competition. He teamed up with a guy named Jake who he met there, and together they did well in team bowling competitions. They competed in doubles two years in a row, and the second year were able win a medal. Devin also participated in Special Olympics basketball.

In April 2017, Donna and I were rocked to our cores as Devin had become so depressed and lonely that he became suicidal, and was to the point he was considering taking actions. He was still seeing his therapist at the time, Miss Tracy, and she raised the flag. I was traveling, and Donna was faced with admitting him into St. Anthony's Medical Center in St Louis, and leaving him there, without me there to help her. After the shock of the first couple days, Devin started liking the fact that he had no decisions to make and had a set routine. While he missed us and missed having his music and his swing, he was comfortable. He stayed about seven days.

Here are the poems he had written up to this point. He got a couple of them published in books at Lewis and Clark College[J, K], where he was a student, and also in the book "Upon Arrival: Triumph"[L]:

What a Nerd

Squares and rectangles
An animal with no tail
You don't have to stand

Get Some Clothes On

I look indecent
I'm wearing no shirt or pants
No socks on my feet
Even though I'm not naked
Some people think otherwise

What's That Noise
A Haiku (17 syllables)

Country, pop, metal
Guitars, pianos, cymbals
I just love music

Imaginary Deception

I want to grab this
It seems I'll be happier
With it beside me

Will it truly bring me joy?
Or is it a fantasy?

What a Sight

They're great to look at
So many different types
Not one is ugly
If nobody can see them
Everyone is blind
I have questions about them
I clearly like them
Not only are they pretty
All colors are wonderful

Highly Frequent Thinness

Small is typical
Large is less than usual
All aluminum
There is no poison involved
Red Bull is commonly short

For Their Sake, Not Yours

Artists of all sorts
Cannot do what pleases them
Fans don't allow it

Is There or Is There Not Paint?

Up above all else
Absolutely not the sky

Not outside either
To be found beyond brick walls
Away from plants, rocks, and trees

Out in the Field

Green under your feet
Yellow and blinding above
Noises from fliers
At no time should you be bit
Scratch yourself no rash either

No Manner of Life Remains

The pipes are empty
Exhaust is present no more
The engine is still
Motion fluid is absent
Functionality is ceased

Dangerous Blueness

Small, white and bubbly
Avoid having your throat stuffed
Where are your two legs?
Push yourself to escape
Move your arms at your top speed

The Excellence of Roundness

Circularity
Hard to seek without finding

Spheres are surprises
If you picture them with care
They are squares without endings
How interesting is that?

Chocolate Chips

Saving and spending
Eating, rolling and squeezing
Dough equals money

It's the Law

Correct and proper
No impossibility
Redeem yourself now
Become a good citizen
You're a criminal
Suffer for your wrongdoings
Miranda is your leader

Mr. Oral
A Tanka (31 syllables)

If I lick at this
I'm going to suck on that
It's time to eat these
I'm drinking those afterward
My tongue, teeth, and jaws need work

Keep it to Yourself

There's a clone of me
Heat and coldness in my hands
I'm sitting on white
Before you see my shadow
I have to take my clothes off

The Cruelty of My Brain

Torture is absent
Bullying is fictional
Fighting isn't real
There's no such thing as warfare
My cranium is heartless

Apparent Abominableness

Have hate for no one
Thoughts of those you detest
Make you one of them

The Waves of Deadly Panic

Nonexistent rest
On the search for cool dryness
White-and-black objects
On your face cannot be closed
The ground is liquid
The heat from over your head
Intolerable

What brought public decency
Is now unaffordable

My Low-Quality Personhood

I have no talent
I have zero confidence
I lack in passion
My heart should be motionless
Why will my life continue?
I want to keep on writing

Regret Comes Easy

Sober expression,
My eyebrows are pointing down
The sides of my lips
Are not curved for enjoyment
No one to visit
In a small room by myself
Walking at random
Or sitting down for a deep thought
After exiting
And then heading miles away
People discomfort
And sadden me rapidly
The first location
Felt more pleasant than the next
I miss what bored me before

Building vs. Breaking

I'm here to help you
What is it that you're thinking?
I lost my boyfriend
Shut up and find someone else
Why'd you have to get so mean?

Foul Filthiness

Workers and dead fish
Green water on the bottom
An offensive place

Why So Proud?

More intelligence,
Freedom, Control, and support
On my side of the small coin

Spare Me All the Duties

Never mind standing
I'm going to sit
Forget walking
I'll just relax without moving
Away with responsibility
On with recreation
Leave me alone
I'm busy not working right now

Conversations

You're not by yourself
There's somebody else with you
Look at each other
Change volume, pitches and tones
Use your words not your actions

What's That From?
A Choka (Alternating 5/7 syllables,
this one 79 syllables total)

Let's watch some TV
It's the S.B. Spongemobile
Like a car model
Hardee's ads anybody?
Women with hoses
Spraying soap off their bodies
Where's SpongeBob going?
Oh wait I remember now
It's from the movie
Where's the road (road, road, road, road)?
Popular culture
Random mentions excite me
Sometimes nonsense has a point

Mortal Kombat

1992
Blue, yellow, and green ninjas
Two in with one out

Gods, red-eyed killers, women,
Movie stars, and monks
Because of these warriors
The inside is the outside

In the Garage

I walk on concrete
Trying to avoid sweating
While I'm wearing green
I don't want to wet my shoes
So I'm walking on bare feet

It Was an Accident

The Ram was a car
On the highway with a bike
Was a teenager
Unable to Dodge the car
He flipped all over the place
He can't talk, hear, see or walk

How Irrelevant

Let's type, write and read
If you like yourself a lot
Congratulations
Even if you're arrogant
That doesn't make you stupid

I Don't Smoke

No marijuana
Everything I see exists
I love Canibus

My Nonexistent Literacy

The Romans and Greeks
Told story after story
All tails have two sides
Little Miss Nicki says so
I enjoy reading, don't you?

My Possible Rudeness

Start clicking your mouse
What's Jack Black's next movie called?
Though this is a gift
You don't need wrapping paper
When I move my tongue
There are times it chaps my lips
Where is your laundry?
Why don't you have a basket?
You don't have a job
You ball things up and throw them
You should join some kind of sport

Wash Your Hands

Let's not be filthy
Remove germs from all fingers
Du hast mich gefragt

Dip It In

Ketchup and mustard
The two of them are awesome
Other types of sauce
Here's an ad with Ray-Ray's dad
Are either okay or bad

Lewey and D'Troy

One who deals cocaine
Another who earns payments
From stolen hubcaps
Both of them are criminals
Neither of them is a saint

Backhanded Complements

For a fat woman
Your face looks very pretty
For an old hobo
You certainly do work hard
You're clean for someone who smells

The Scariness Is Over

This is no movie
The panic room is empty
No more worrying
Don't fear anything further
Take the time to calm yourself

What's Necessary Doesn't Last Forever

All of your teammates
You shouldn't doubt they love you
And here's the reason
If they had no such feelings
They wouldn't surround you now
Take their love with gratitude

High There

These don't flap at all
Nor can anyone eat them
You won't get cancer
And no metal falls on you
Take not in or out
No sirens will be blaring
Up here in the sky
What the attendants bring you
Insert into your torso

Not What It Looks Like

You feel it's your life
Appearing on the surface
Your environment
It looks like reality
You're not in your world
In another dimension
You're playing no sports
No scoring, no goals, no points
Still you have to shoot
If you don't fire what you hold
Away with your existence

Won't You Take Me With You?

Don't rush yourself now
If you don't slow down at all
You'll truly feel it
Wait, what do you mean by that?
Speed can't be that bad
Not all hurries are harmful
Sometimes they're needed
I'm headed to the track now
Father ought to run with me

No Logical Motive

What are you doing?
Why are we here together?
Much more of a bond

You claim that's what you desire
You share your feelings
Yes, you should care about mine
Why is it right now?
Why did you not ask before?
Boy are you busy
I'm preoccupied as well
I'm not paid for it
It's not an obligation
It's entertainment
Don't worry what I'm doing
It's what I enjoy
If you don't cause me trouble
I won't make problems for you

Is It My Birthday?[J]

Miles, feet, inches, yards
I'm already using mine
No goals to achieve
My day has been so easy
I've been walking in the park

Not in My Eyes but In My Mind[K]

I used to see them
Neither drawings nor paintings
Supernatural
That wasn't the case either
Yet they haunted me

Although this was no movie
They were directors
I like controlling my thoughts
Thank goodness I have that skill

Solid Tenderness[(L)]

You stab your mattress
And feathers begin to fly
Is it Matricide?

Mr. I-Don't-Read's Alliterative Irony

Jacob Joseph Jay unjustly murdered by Jeffrey Ja
Seth Sullivan Sam is stupid, silly and stuck up
Insanely interested in ink, IDs, and dry ice
Rigid Randy Richard Roberts is ready to rumble in the ring
Marvelous Mysterious Master Mitchell will mark the
mighty end
Goodbye, you great, graceful, grand, gorgeous, gracious
ladies and gentlemen

Donna found a program called Social School, in Edwardsville. This was a once a week program, focused on one-on-one interaction, and coaching, to put the student into social situations, and work with them on responses, and building confidence. Coming out of this program, Devin began to make small talk, which he could never do before. Jesse does a great job in this program.

Donna researched and found out about a Junior College special needs program in Godfrey, Illinois, at Lewis and Clark Community College. We toured the campus, and found the people to be wonderful. Even though it was about 65 miles from the house, Devin enrolled, and Donna drove him there two to three times a week. It was too far to come home, so she would wait there. After the first semester, she enrolled in a class, too, to occupy some time. Just think about it, though. Here is a guy with autism, that couldn't even speak for more than two years of his life, now taking college classes. He was absolutely amazing.

Devin developed a very funny response if he didn't want to do something. Instead of just saying no, he would say "Sure, what time?" then before you had a chance to answer, "No thanks." He would use this frequently, and get a chuckle out of us each time.

Devin had always struggled with restaurants and long waits. When he was really young, the issue was his food limitations. Many times we would carry a McDonald's bag into the Chinese or Mexican restaurant with us, so he could eat. As he became older, the issue was noise sensitivity. If a child in the room was screaming or laughing loudly, he would completely shut down. In more recent years, we found ways to help, such as letting him pick songs on a juke box, or giving him a $20 bill to play the slot machines (something he was quite lucky at), or just playing tic-tac-toe or connect four on my phone while we waited.

In May 2017, Lindsey came up from Kentucky and took Devin on a day out in St. Louis. They went to the arch, and to the city museum, and out for a burger. He was excited to ride the Ferris wheel up on the roof of the museum. Lindsey has always had a close connection with Devin, and in fact, went into a career in special education because of him.

In June 2017, a large group of us went to see Metallica at Busch Stadium, home of the St. Louis Cardinals. Devin was always afraid to try things like this because he might not be able to handle it and then would disappoint others if he had to leave. At first he declined, but a week before the show, when he found out who all was going, and when I agreed that if it was too much, we would leave, and by getting him some foam ear plugs, and a pair of shooting-range ear muffs, I was able to convince him to go along. He ended up having a blast, and only needed the ear plugs. That day was an intense downpour, so we all got ponchos in the gift shop. Our tickets were floor access, general admission, so we stood for about six hours, but we all had a great time. I wish I had convinced him to go to see Kid Rock when he was in town.

*On the floor at the Metallica concert during a pause in the rain.
left to right, me, Devin, Brad and Kyle*

Devin in his Metallica shirt

In November 2017, Kullen moved back in with us in Highland. He and Devin became close again. They watched many funny shows together, like stand-up comedies on Netflix, South Park, or Tosh.0. They also played video games, and just hung out together a couple hours every day. Kullen was such a great friend for Devin.

There were many good times and family gatherings while we lived in Highland, like the Halloween when a group of the guys all dressed up like Super Mario characters, or when Kullen and his friends came up to go to a German restaurant for his birthday.

Kyle, Kullen, Jeff and Devin in their Mario costumes

Halloween at Mark and Debbie's

Kullen's birthday at Roemer Topf
Left to right, Devin, Tim, Kyle, Kullen

*At Lotawata Creek Left to right, Donna, Chad,
Judy, Jerry, Brad, Jeff, Tracy, Sierra, Devin*

Devin was always researching things on the
computer. He found out about Rotten Tomatoes, where
people pick the worst movies. This led to the Angry
Video Game Nerd, and ultimately, his favorite, the
Nostalgia Critic. This YouTube channel features a very
funny guy who reviews old movies and tears them apart,
yelling and throwing things. After Devin would watch
these episodes, he would want to watch the movie, to see
if it was really that bad.

Although he was a daredevil, he could never talk
himself into trying a roller coaster. He did regret not
buying a ticket for the crazy one atop the Stratosphere,
though. He would spend lots of time researching the
best, fastest, tallest and craziest coasters, and we would

talk about them. He wanted to see them in person, but didn't want to ride them.

Later in 2017, we started Devin in piano lessons at Melodic Rhythms, in Belleville, Illinois. His instructor was Gary McClain. A few weeks into lessons, Gary asked Devin to sing along to a basic song like "Twinkle Twinkle Little Star." After the lesson he asked Donna if we would be okay with Devin taking singing lessons, while also learning piano. Gary is an incredible instructor, who brings out the best in his students, and works hard to arrange venues for the students to showcase their talents. Devin performed in front of crowds five times, and you could see his confidence growing with each experience. He sang these songs on stage spectacularly:

➢ "Imagine" by John Lennon

➢ "Yellow, and Trouble" by Coldplay

➢ "Down in the Valley" by Pete Seeger

➢ "What a Wonderful World" by Louis Armstrong

➢ "Happy Together" by the Turtles

➢ "I Guess That's Why They Call It The Blues" by Elton John

➢ "Chasing Cars" by Snow Patrol

There were many other songs he would sing in the practice sessions with Gary. As he got more comfortable, he began working on singing "Imagine" while playing his own piano accompaniment. He was extremely talented. As proud parents, we thoroughly enjoyed seeing this quiet, calm, loving guy, up on stage, singing his heart out. Most of the family loved to watch him sing, especially his grandma, Judy. She always said he was so talented and just needed to be noticed.

In late 2017, we came upon a once-in-a-lifetime opportunity to buy a unique, architect-designed, house with water on two sides on Carlyle Lake. These homes typically stay in families for generations, and so are never available. Some friends of ours, Dave and Cindy, were retiring to Hilton Head and offered it to us. We did some research about other community colleges, and other places to work. We took some time to think about it.

Devin started his second season of Special Olympics basketball, but unfortunately, in December 2017 he had another bout of ITP. He was treated with IVIG and Rituxan. It took until March 2018 to get his platelets to stay above 50,000, and he had to withdraw from the team. The puzzling thing was that it had been seven years since his first bout. We had not moved and really hadn't changed anything in terms of school or medicine. The only thing unique was joining basketball and being exposed to a lot more people.

Right after New Years 2018, Alex came and spent a few days with Devin. We were still living in Highland at the time. Devin was excited to go to the movies with Alex without mom or dad.

In March 2018, we bought the house and moved to Carlyle. The biggest advantage on the list was that

Devin would get a crack at having his own place to live, as he would be in the trailer we'd owned for a few years. Despite having autism, Devin transitioned with no issue. In fact, he did very well at Kaskaskia College, making the dean's list for part-time students. The only problem he had with this school vs. the one in Godfrey was that here he felt invisible. No students ever spoke to him.

We had purchased an older Jeep Wrangler about a year before moving to Carlyle. Devin loved to ride around in it, especially when the roof was removed. I made a playlist that had a few of his rap songs on it, so within a few minutes he would be smiling, as we cruised around. There were probably 50 nights he and I, and sometimes Donna, would go for a ride, just to get out. One night in Carlyle, it was about 70 degrees out, and we decided to take a ride and get a Dairy Queen Blizzard. We decided to eat there. When we left the sun had gone down and the temperature had dropped, and we were freezing on the way home, even with the heater on full blast. He laughed the whole way home.

As I mentioned, Devin never wanted to disappoint anyone. One challenge he had was Mathlab. This was a website where math students could spend time doing extra work, to be sure they understood things. His issue was that he would work weeks ahead based on the class syllabus, and would sacrifice fun time with family and friends, as he would be worried about doing his math work.

In the first few months after we moved there, my bother Chad was around some, playing games with Devin. They connected remotely on Nintendo Switch too. Chad ended up getting a different job and had less time to hang out and play games. Devin also lost some interest in playing Switch online, which made connecting more of a challenge.

When a rap song would come on, Devin could tell you about the history of the song, the beef between the different rappers, where they got their start, and anything else you could imagine. He spent countless hours researching these things. His love for this genre was incredible. If he was ever in a quiet or down mood, I could turn on a song by Eminem, and he would start rocking in his seat and smiling.

Devin always wanted to be famous. He thought maybe a rapper or a DJ. We got him a basic DJ setup for his birthday in 2018 and a new laptop to manage the songs and software. It turned out to be not really what he had envisioned. It was more about mixing and fading music together. He really wasn't interested. In fact, when I would ask him to be the DJ at a party or on the boat, he would grab the phone, navigate to songs, hit shuffle, then hit play. He honestly loved all music, and didn't care what was on; he found it all wonderful.

In June 2018, Devin had another bout of ITP. Donna and I were at an annual event with customers and had to catch emergency flights home to get to the hospital, where Kullen had taken Devin for us. It took IVIG and several rounds of Rituxan treatment to get his platelets back to a safe level. As we look back now on these bouts, and compare his with Donna's, we realize that the hospital never did a CT scan to see if Devin was bleeding internally. They also never did more than one dose of IVIG. Something else we've found is that between his second and third bouts, his platelets never really got back to the safe minimum level above 150,000. I've charted his platelets around the time of these bouts and included this in Appendix 3. Looking back, this bout was really an extension of the one that started in December of 2017.

After being off work for a few months, Devin got a job at Community Link in Breese, Illinois. This is a fantastic organization that gives people with disabilities the chance to learn job skills and contribute to society. It is a sub-minimum-wage, not-for-profit environment, where the family actually provides funding to the company, and they in turn provide the wages, and skills training. He liked working in this environment because they understood him and his needs and challenged him, but only to the level he could handle. He felt cared for and valued. After working there for a few months, though, he asked not to go to any more ICA events, because, in his words "I've been with disabled people all day, I'd rather be with normal people in the evening." As always, Donna was Devin's primary driver for this, too, but he actually preferred when she was busy, so our friend Karen could give him rides.

In late summer 2018, Devin's Grandma Judy found out she had stage 4 cancer. It was seen all over her liver, coming from the pancreas. This came as a huge blow to the whole family, especially Devin, as she was one of his biggest fans. She was strong. She always said, "We all have a date, and when it's your turn, there's no reason to fuss over it." Her side of the family had all the strange disorders like lupus and multiple sclerosis, so she was expecting something strange to get her, not cancer. Her fight didn't last long, as after her first treatment, she suffered a major stroke, and by late September, she had passed. A couple months after her passing, we got together at our place in Carlyle, to just relax and not think about it.

Playing Cards Against Humanity
Left to right. Me, Brad, Chad, Jerry, Devin and Donna

Devin expanded his interest in poetry. He would research different forms, and the number of syllables per line or for the total poem, then come up with a poem to fit that form. He also wrote quite a few poems and emailed most them to me and Donna, and we would ask him questions about what he was thinking when he was creating them. We were very proud of this amazing talent.

The Correct Form of Playfulness

I am a master
Payments I will always make
All copies of me in stacks
Giving leaflets is inadequate
Sobriety hated by jesters
Pulling and playing both available
What friends have brought to them
Costly and expensive
Dangerous, hazardous, and risky

Acceptance vs. Decline

What I love not hate
My likes not dislikes
Do what is pleasing
Think what is satisfying
Say what is comfortable
Remember yes
Forget no

Forced In Without Exclusion

Place them on your palm
Leave them sit on your hand
Insert them into your grasp
Have a hold of them
Hang on without letting go
They're your prisoners
So never release

Meeting Our Demise

Welcome to earthquakes
Everybody catches fire
I hope you like toast
You all come into contact
Or lasers are shot
Doom, Quake, Hexen, Heretic
Childhood enjoyment
Prior to adolescence
I pushed and shoved my way through

Ceasing to Function

Reaching the conclusion
Meeting the termination
Having lasted until the halt
Once that has happened to you
Welcome to the cemetery
Or here you have your ashes
Let's hope you were fond of your existence

Giving Myself Shaky Hugs

No hands on shoulders
No self-congratulating
Arms around my ribs
Chilling is not done to me
I am just weeping
And I am also trembling
Awkwardness makes me quiver

Look at Me

Wrapping a belt around your neck
Just not actually tying it
Who doesn't want attention?

Banging your fists on the floor
And kicking the tiles while down
Who doesn't need publicity?

Exposing your teeth,
Spreading your lips,
Hurting cheekbones,
And amusing others
Who doesn't enjoy being given heed?

My Solitary Specialty

Distancing myself
Refraining from appearing
Concealing my face

Secreting both of my eyes
Avoidance is essential
Privacy I have asked for

I'll Give You a Letter

Don't forget your cap
Rays, shine, and light there will be
Don't leave it open
That door was made to be shut
Are you on the phone?
Don't be calling for too long
Get out of my zone
Comfort is necessary
But find a place for yourself

Squashing of Beef

Making hamburgers
The shortness of your birth name
Grinning and smirking
I'm going to tickle you
And I'll make you start tingling

A Paradoxical Contradiction

Not too long ago
There was an ironic name
And a melody
Someone else was by his side
Future in the front

A four-year-old recording
I heard Lil Wayne too
The main artist is Future
Yet the song is from the past

The Blows of Criminal Grisliness

Shi Kaga is a felon
Is he in a gang?
Does he kill?

Take it to NE
1-2-3-4-1 Syllable Poem

What
It was
Was protest
No party at
All

In December 2018, after nearly five years on a wait list, Devin was selected for the Illinois Prioritization for Urgency of Need for Services (PUNS) program. This Medicaid waiver program was wonderful, as it provided funding for services, such as Community Link where he worked, but also for Community Integrated Living Arrangements (CILAS) such as group homes, and for Personal Service Workers (PSW), to help individuals learn life skills. Joe became Devin's first PSW on the program, coming up once a week for a few hours to go to dinner and bowling, or to watch movies. Joe ended up getting serious with a girlfriend, so these times fizzled out after a couple months, but they were great while they lasted.

The challenge for parents of children with special needs is that programs like PUNS are not advertised or promoted to let you know they are available. If you don't know someone who has received the benefit, you may never know it exists. In our case, my cousin, Brian, and his wife Denise have a daughter with special needs, so they helped us figure it out. In my opinion, parents must constantly dig for these types of programs, and advocate for their children, because the state is fine with letting them fall through the cracks if you don't.

I mentioned we moved to Carlyle in 2018. We ordered a second swing set from Component Playgrounds, so Devin could enjoy swinging without having to go over to the park. All the neighbors got to know him as the guy who was always out in the yard swinging. Alex came for a visit that August, and spent a few days in the trailer with Devin, and on the water with us.

Devin's confidence was growing in many ways. Not only could he handle public speaking and singing, but he could change jobs, change schools, move to another town, and keep on trucking. In many ways, Devin's final year was his happiest. He was able to spend lots of time with Kullen, and with Kullen's friends, Matt and Steve. They would come hang with him, take him bowling, play video games, watch movies, or play Devin's favorite, Cards Against Humanity. Devin was able to truly enjoy the time with them, but after they would leave, his depression would return.

Alex came to visit again over Christmas, and he and Devin seemed as though they had never been apart. As much as Devin enjoyed time with family and other friends, Alex was always that one constant in his life. When they were together, they were content. They could just hang out, and have a great time doing it.

Devin encountered bullying again, this time at Kaskaskia College. Recall the social skills program with Jesse from earlier? Well, a girl in one of Devin's classes had a new computer, and Devin was going to talk about it with her, before class started, just to make small talk. He asked her about it, and she ignored him. He tapped her on the shoulder to ask again, thinking she didn't hear him, and she jerked away to face her friends. He cried in the car on the way home, wondering why she wouldn't even talk to him.

Devin decided he would try alcohol. He had avoided it most of his life, mainly because he had heard about hangovers. He liked the confidence it gave him. He could say some things a bit more risky than he normally would. One time, while playing Cards Against Humanity, April, a friend of the family, was judging, and her card was "My teacher was surprised when I ___" and when she read Devin's answer card, "Licked my own nipple," Devin said out loud to the group, "please do that" and the whole group erupted in laughter. Having autism, Devin began to try every combination of mixed drink he could come up with. He also took a liking to moscato and other sweet wines.

In spring 2019, we worked with Dr. Shenoy to do some experimenting to see if maybe some of his condition or treatment could be causing his depression. In March, Devin had a lumbar puncture at Barnes Hospital. He got a spinal fluid leak and had to get an epidural blood patch the next day. The leak caused horrible headaches for a few days. He also had an EEG and an MRI, and when I texted him to ask about the tests, his reply said "During the EEG, I had stickers on my chest and my head. Afterwards, during the MRI, I had to lie down with some headphones, and I had a cage on my face. Then my head went into a tunnel, and I got to listen to '80s rock music." In April, we switched from Prednisone, which he had been on for about 22 years, to hydrocortisone, to see if maybe the Prednisone could be causing some of the depression. There was no real benefit from any of these tests.

In May 2019, Devin performed in a recital at a church in Belleville. He sang a medley of Coldplay songs. As usual, he was fantastic. That month, he also got to go to a St Louis Cardinal's game with the Community Link crew. He didn't care for the game but was a big fan of the concessions and getting out of work.

Devin asked to have a birthday party at Dave & Busters that same month. Kullen, Matt and Steve went with us, and Darren and Celine met us there. He made a night of it! He was all about the video games and the basketball games. He enjoyed the dinner and drinks, as well.

Donna was always looking for things she and Devin could do, especially on weeknights, when I would typically be traveling for work. One of these things turned out to be the Looking Glass Playhouse in Lebanon, Illinois. This is a small town local performing arts venue, where volunteers perform popular plays. Devin loved to get out of the house. I'm thinking he preferred the dinner and the snacks at the playhouse more than the play itself, but nonetheless this became a date night for the two of them several times a year. I would join them whenever I was in town. One of Devin's favorites was "The Rocky Horror Picture Show."

The summer of 2019, Devin started to boat with us more. He still didn't care much for sunscreen or lake water but enjoyed when Kullen brought out his friends, as he could once again laugh, as people failed when attempting to wakeboard for the first time. Some of Kullen's friends also happened to be cute girls, which Devin didn't mind at all. There are numerous funny stories, like the time we got the ski rope wrapped-up into the lower unit, and had to spend time pulling the prop while the boat was full of people, anxious to go boarding.

We spent lots of time on the boat that summer. Devin enjoyed cruising and listening to music, and especially our stops at the Fish House for dinner.

Devin sitting outside the Fish House August 2019

In August 2019, Devin performed three songs, "Happy Together" by the Turtles, "I Guess That's Why They Call It the Blues" by Elton John, and "Chasing Cars" by Snow Patrol at Crehan's Irish Pub in Belleville. There were about 100 people in attendance. As usual, he was spectacular. A large group of family and friends were there, cheering him on.

Later that month, after several months of searching, Donna had found a couple of college students to come meet with Devin, and begin being personal service workers, funded by PUNs. Unfortunately, they never got to the point that they were able to spend time with Devin, due to unexpected issues.

Chapter 4
THE FINAL DAYS
——

Sunday, September 1

Kullen's birthday is September 2nd, so it always lands on or near the Labor Day holiday. The year 2019 was no different. We had a large group of people out for a day of boating on Sunday, the first, then a day of swimming, and grilling, on Monday the second. We set out on the boat Sunday, and Devin was in his usual spot, to my left, in the co-captain's chair. Devin noticed some spots on his left hand shortly after we got out of our cove, and asked if it was petechiae. I couldn't see anything. Donna took a look and did see what could be very a mild case coming on. We decided to watch and see. We all had a good day hanging out.

Monday, September 2

The next morning, I ran to the store to get a few last minute things for the day of swimming and grilling. I crossed paths with Donna and Devin at the stop sign in our subdivision. We rolled windows down, and she said, "ITP is back." Devin stuck out his tongue and from my vehicle. I could see the blisters. Donna said to continue with the plans for the day, and she would take him for a blood test to get the counts.

Later that day, we got the results, and his platelets were at 1,000. Normal range is 150,000 to 350,000. Donna had to take him to Children's Hospital so they could admit him and give him IVIG and Rituxan. He needed to stay for 24 hours to be sure there were no reactions.

Tuesday, September 3

Devin typically enjoyed hospital stays because, similar to when he was flying, there were no decisions to make. The problem this time was that he was in children's hospital, so there was lots of crying and he couldn't handle it. He asked if he could go home, and the doctors said that since this wasn't his first case, and we knew that he responded well to IVIG and Rituxan, he could go home, but he was not to exert himself – no stairs, etc. – but could go to school if he wanted. We conceded and brought him home. Even at this extremely low platelet level, the hospital did no CT scan to ensure there was no internal bleeding.

Wednesday, September 4

This was a typical day for us. After I got off work, we had our normal dinner together. Devin was sitting at the table, and his nose started to bleed. This was not uncommon. He had frequent nose bleeds over the years.

This one was a very intense, heavy bleed, which was not like his normal nose bleeds. After about 15 minutes, we called the hospital and paged the on-call hematologist, she told us that as long as it stops in the next 10 minutes, or so, this and headaches are not uncommon with these medicines, and recommended an ice pack on the back of the neck. We were able to get it to stop, eat dinner, and watch a movie together.

Thursday, September 5

This day was shaping up the same. I was grilling dinner under the gazebo. Donna and Devin walked up and asked what I thought about him swinging. I said a full swing was a bad idea due to the associated pressure changes, but it would be ok to gently rock back and forth. When dinner was ready, Devin came back over and we were grabbing food and heading to our seats in the living room. He dropped his napkin, and when he leaned over to get it, I stopped him, and said I'd get it, but it was too late, he already had grabbed around his left temple and said ouch. He was smiling after, so this, plus the doctors saying headaches were normal, didn't set off any alarms. After the show, which was only about 8 p.m., he said he was tired and wanted to call it a night, and if we were okay with it, he would stay with us. Both of these were not like Devin, but we knew he was fatigued from the ITP, and not feeling himself due to the medicines.

Friday, September 6

At 3 a.m., we heard the ice maker. Donna opened our door upstairs and stepped out onto the balcony, and asked if he was okay. He said he was, and that he just needed some ice for the sores in his mouth. Everything seemed fine.

At 5:30 a.m., he texted Donna stating "I can only move my left arm and left leg. My right arm and my right leg are numb." She ran down to check on him, and called 911. I was just settling into the gym for my normal morning exercise program, when the urgent texts came through. I rushed home, and got there in time that Devin was still awake enough to say hi. Within minutes, while I was running around listening to the policewoman telling me to gather medicine and clothes, he was no longer able to speak.

The ambulance got lost but finally arrived then loaded him up and took him to the hospital in Breese. There they did a CT scan, and the doctor said he had a massive brain bleed. Donna asked for the worst case, and she said there was a real possibility he would not survive. They put him into the medical helicopter and sent him to Children's Hospital. We arrived about the same time as he did.

Devin had to go through another CT scan, and some other checks, and ended up in the Pediatric Intensive Care Unit, around 9:30 a.m. We met with the Pediatric Neurosurgery team, and they explained to us that Devin had a profoundly-life-threatening injury, and that they were going to involve us in every decision, and do everything they could to try to save him, but it was very likely he would not survive. The CT scan showed that his brain had swelled to the right, shifting everything off-center, and also herniated downward, compressing his brain stem.

The head surgeon said this was the first time in his 12 years doing this that he was faced with this dilemma – he needed to open the skull immediately to relieve pressure, but Devin only had 1,000 platelets, and so would most likely bleed-out and die on the operating table. The plan of attack was to give an N-plate injection and bags of platelets every hour, then check his counts. We needed him to get above 100,000 to meet hospital protocol for the craniotomy. Each bag of platelets contains millions, and it's not uncommon for someone's count to jump hundreds of thousands after a single bag is infused.

The hospital reserved its conference room for our family for that day, so we could all stay together, away from the normal waiting room area, and close when they needed us. They also bent some rules and brought in a second bed-chair so that Donna and I could both stay with Devin every night.

We were approaching noon, and Devin's platelets were around 25,000. The issue was that his spleen was killing the platelets almost as fast as we were adding them. They decided it was worth the risk to do an emergency splenectomy with platelets at about half the normal target level, so the spleen could no longer destroy the added platelets. At about 12:30, they took him back and removed his spleen. They also shaved his head and prepped him for the craniotomy, in case his platelets would climb and allow the surgery.

At about 2 p.m. they came out and said he survived the splenectomy, but his platelets didn't climb and so held-off doing the craniotomy. We challenged this, asking why we could do one but not the other. In the case of the splenectomy, if something happened, they could push against ribs to stop the bleeding. In the case of the craniotomy, you can't press the brain against anything.

We went back to the routine of adding platelets every hour. By about 4 p.m., his eyes stopped responding to light. Dr. Shenoy came in to see us. She was on vacation and getting ready to head out on a safari, but wanted to talk with us. She believed at that point his ALPS was kicking in, and his liver was now doing what the spleen had been doing before. She said there may be no stopping it this time.

At about 6 p.m., Devin's heart began to race, and got between 150 and 180 beats per minute, and stayed there for several hours. At around 9 p.m., the head surgeon called us together and said Devin's brain is under so much pressure that the body is reacting, and if we don't do anything, he will expire in a matter of a few more hours. His platelets were only about 45,000, but they were willing to try the craniotomy if we agreed, as the latest EEG showed there was still some brain activity on the right side. I told Donna that doing this surgery could ultimately lead us to a point we'd be faced with a decision to remove life support, and made sure she understood before we said yes. We got the whole family together, and all agreed we had to try.

Before they took him back, as a just in case, they brought in an ultrasound, and recorded his heart beat for us. Devin was prepped and taken back for surgery. We moved out to the conference room to wait with our support group. Beating the odds again, Devin had survived this surgery too!

September 7 to 19

At about 12:30 a.m. on the 7th, the head surgeon again pulled us together and said that Devin had survived the surgery, but when they removed the section of skull, and the clot came out, some brain matter came out with it. There's no way to know what part of the brain, but they had to cut it off and staple the skin back together over the opening.

The infusion of platelets continued overnight. In fact, a total of 24 bags were given, depleting the entire supply the hospital had on hand.

We were relieved that he had survived the surgery. There was no way to know how much he would recover, if any, until the brain swelling subsided. This could be several days. We settled into a routine of meeting with the team in the hall each morning for rounds, discussing how he was doing, and what next steps would be. The first day or two after the surgery, Devin was breathing one or two more breaths per minute than the ventilator was forcing. He was struggling to maintain his blood glucose levels, his urine sodium levels, and his body temperature, all of which were signs his brain stem had sustained damage.

For the next several days, we were along for the ride, and helping as much as they would let us. I would help turn him so they could clean and change him, and Donna would help with bathing and oral hygiene. We setup a link on Caring Bridge, a wonderful website where you can invite people to share stories, etc., while keeping them up to date on how things are going. This can be a big help for those on the front lines, as they are torn between focusing on the patient, listening to the medical staff, and keeping everyone on the outside updated.

As I mentioned, we had team Devin with us the whole time. They visited in rotating shifts, some sleeping in the family break room. We also had many other visitors. Sam and Lori, our long-time friends from Mascoutah came to pray over Devin, as did Pastor Duane from Mascoutah First Baptist Church, and Pastor Josh from Carlyle Christian Church. Cole and Jessica, our good friends from the lake, came by a couple times, to visit and to bring us some food and drinks. My cousin

Brian and his wife Denise also came to see us. My co-worker, Vicki, came up to see us one day, too. She and some other co-workers pitched in and sent us gift cards for use in the hospital cafeteria, which we thought was a really creative idea, and have since done ourselves for others in the hospital.

Remember how I started this book noting that I'd had two dreams that were like visions? The Wednesday after the stroke, on the 11th, I woke up after having a horrible dream, and decided I needed to tell people about it. I told my brother Jeff first, then told Donna. In this dream, it was completely peaceful, almost silent. I was laying on my left side facing Devin, and Donna was on her right side facing him. We were all in the same bed, and Devin had passed away. I told her at that moment I believed he would not be coming home with us. Not that I was going to give up, but it felt very real to me.

My cousin Mike stopped by a couple times on his way home from work. During one of these visits, we were outside Devin's room looking through the window, and Mike said something that stuck with me. He said that most people don't realize that what we were going through at that moment was life. I thought about this for a while, and believe he is correct. I used to believe life was all about the good times, but it is really about facing devastating events and finding ways to survive.

We continued the fight for another week, or so, and then became faced with some horrible news. Without the ventilator, Devin would take no breaths at all. He still could not control sugar, sodium or temperature, and could also not digest any of the food they tried giving down his tube. The head of the department, Dr. Celeste, was incredible. She sat with us several times, and talked about these tough decisions. Her family had been through similar. She showed us, by going through five of the seven brain-death tests, that he was, in fact, brain dead. Kullen was in the room with us during the tests. I struggled with this brain dead assessment because he still showed reflex motions, etc. I told her that I would not believe it without EEG and MRI evidence.

The next day, they did another EEG. I was not in the room at the time, as some folks from our old church in Mascoutah were visiting, so didn't get to do the test I wanted to do – squeeze his fingernail to get a reflex, and prove to me the brain isn't involved, but nonetheless, the EEG showed zero brain activity. They also took him for an MRI, which they rarely do in these cases. The result was something almost impossible to even explain. The team of doctors called it the worst MRI they had ever seen. Nothing in the brain was where it was supposed to be, it didn't have the normal snake-like shapes you see in brain images, rather it looked as if someone had put their fingers in it and stretched it in all directions, and despite being at about 150,000 platelets, there was another brain bleed happening in a different location at the time! The team of doctors all agreed there was nothing left we could do. We asked if they would support us if we went for second opinions, and they agreed.

For the next couple days we researched the best places around the country for brain trauma, and only found one that would look at the EEG and MRI and give an opinion. The other two, because he was unresponsive, would not talk with us. The one reached back out to us, and said they concur that with the MRI they saw, there was no hope.

Obviously, we were broken. We decided to sleep on it. The next morning, we both woke up with the realization that we were going to have to make a decision to remove life support. We met with Dr. Celeste and team and told them we could not be the ones to decide on a date to do it, they understood and then offered Friday, Sept. 20, at noon, in the rooftop garden, and we agreed. After this, we started backing off the medications, and the daily rounds became less intense.

On one of these mornings, I sat with Donna and we talked about how we would never be the same, and that I believed the only way we could possibly survive would be to get every type of counselling – individual, couples, and group.

We had a couple of days to go, and it felt like a death-row sentence. We knew that by the end of the week, we would no longer have his hands to hold. The hospital brought in a palliative care team, and they created some memory keepsakes, like thumb- and hand-prints of Devin, Devin and Kullen, and the four of us.

Friday, September 20

The worst day of our lives had arrived. As we woke, we knew this would be the last morning we would ever get to see our son. My boss flew in from Connecticut, just to give us each a hug, then headed back. Before flying home, he participated in a 1-hour prayer conference call with my staff and others, from noon to 1 p.m., while we were to be in the garden.

Our family and friends were all in the ICU. About 15 of us filled Devin's room and the corridor outside his door. At noon, they led us up to the rooftop garden. It was a beautiful warm day, with partly cloudy skies and a gentle breeze. The wind chimes were playing peacefully for us. Everyone had their chance to say their final respects, then the chaplain led us in a service. After that, we turned on recordings of Devin singing, and Donna and I climbed into Devin's bed and held him as they stopped the manual bag ventilation. I was on my left side, Donna on her right side, exactly as I had seen it in my dream. In a matter of about five minutes, he passed. Aside from a stiffening in his extremities, it was totally peaceful. The whole time, we were right there with him, letting him know it was okay. A white butterfly fluttered around, as we laid there with him.

Saturday, September 21

We had a small gathering at Moll Funeral Home in Mascoutah. About 40 close friends and family came to say farewell. Tim from our church family led a small service, and people took turns telling stories.

Saturday, October 26

We had a celebration of life for Devin at the Knights of Columbus hall in Breese, Illinois. The room was set up with food and eating area off to the left. The rest of the room was divided into sections, or stations, for which our friend Gary made some "almost professional" banners to help people navigate. One was looping a video collage I put together showing photos and videos of his life. Another was looping his live singing performances, and was later switched to a collage of his favorite comedy movie clips that Darren pulled together. Another was poster boards showing all his travels. The other two were his favorite video games and board games setup so people could play. We also hung up on the wall the two T-shirt blankets that Mema made for us. Anne was managing a station in the middle, handing out CDs of his singing, and bookmarks explaining ITP and ALPS for everyone to take with them. The core group all wore matching Team Devin t-shirts that we had made at Custom Ink.

Gary from Melodic Rhythms, Devin's cousin Kyle, and Aunt Debbie, sang songs. Devin's friend Alex, cousin Lindsey, Community Link Project Manager, Chris, and family friends, Mema and Christy, stood and talked about what Devin meant to them. I then stood with Donna as she read a wonderful speech she had written.

We were together for four hours, and about 250 people joined us that day. Our extended family was there. My co-workers Vicki and Lalitha came up from Tennessee, and Jeremy came down from Connecticut. My friend and former co-worker, Kishen, came down from Michigan. There were people from ICA, Community Link, and Kaskaskia College, along with friends from, Highland, Carlyle and Smyrna, and many family members in attendance.

Chapter 5

REFLECTIONS

———

I spent some time with Donna, reflecting on Devin's very short life, thinking about some things we regret, some other things we are thankful for, and some key lessons we learned.

We know we can't live our lives focused on what could have been, and that thinking about these things can't change the outcome. But it's almost impossible not to spend time there. As we think about life in general, we regret not keeping him in church, regardless his struggles. We do know that he didn't have the mental capacity to understand decisions, and believe he has gone on to heaven, but believe that keeping him in church would have given him more happiness in this life. We also regret all the moves we made over the years, as we believe some of those moves could have contributed to his conditions – recall him crawling on carpet that had been sprayed for bugs in Columbia, developing OCD due to the militant approach at the middle school in Smyrna, getting ITP for the first time after moving him back to Illinois when he really wanted to stay in Tennessee, and being exposed to added bug sprays after we moved to Carlyle. We also regret contributing to his anxiety as we listened to the schools, and tried to help Devin conform to society, when what we should have been doing was working with society to accept him as he was.

As great as vacations are, we have some regrets about them, too. He always wanted to see New York City, and we never took him. When we were in Paris, Devin really wanted to go up in the Eifel tower. We got to the landing, and then got in line to go to the top, and he got scared. I let him talk himself out of going. He was disappointed later that he didn't do it. In 2019, we had planned a trip to the beach in FL, and Steve was going to join us. We canceled our plans, as we were focused on selling our house in Highland, Illinois. We didn't take a vacation that year, and now don't have the chance to take him on vacation again.

Specific to ITP, we regret not switching him to Dr Greco (Donna's ITP doctor) when we had the chance a few years ago. He was much more conservative in approach, not letting her leave the hospital with low platelets, and doing CT scans any time platelets get down to 1,000. We met with him after Devin passed, and he said that he would have pushed the neurosurgeons to move earlier, as the platelets that remain are new, and are therefore larger and stickier than others. Although he did say that this very well may have been Devin's fait accompli, something that's predetermined and you just have to accept it. Also, a few years ago we discussed doing a splenectomy as a preventative measure but decided against it due to the associated risks of living without a spleen. We regret not spending the time to study the frequency of his bouts to see if it was getting worse, and consider doing this.

I mentioned before that we are not certain what triggered Devin's ITP bouts, but we have found something worth further investigation. In each of Devin's final three bouts, his Lithium Carbonate or Clomipramine dosage changed. We are still digging for exact dates, but looking back at notes from doctor visits, we see that the visit prior to the bout and the visit after the bout, dosages are different. You can see these details in Appendix 3.

In regards to his final ITP battle, we regret listening to the doctors and letting him come home after his IVIG and Rituxan treatments. We also regret not taking him back to the hospital after the massive nose bleed and headaches. Looking back at the night before his stroke, we regret not spending more time in his face trying to understand if he was feeling worse than in his prior bouts. The morning of his stroke, I should have stayed right by Devin while he could still see me instead of listening to the police officer and packing to follow the ambulance. At least Donna stayed close, although on the phone with the EMTs, until they arrived. And finally, as we look back at his final battle with ITP, we regret not having been much stronger advocates, better understanding ITP and drug interactions before this hit him.

But as I mentioned, this does not mean that all we have are regrets. There are many reasons we are thankful.

As we think about our life with Devin and his life in general, we're thankful that he was in our life, even for such a short time, as he totally changed our perspective on the world. We're also thankful that even though he had issues, he was able to walk and talk and live on his own, and travel, and love, and have a sense of humor, and enjoy some things about life. When we think about what he dealt with and what could have happened, we're thankful he didn't have to suffer through lymphoma or other ALPS-related diseases, and that he didn't have to deal with COVID-19, as he was immune-compromised, and would have been very high risk. And while it's hard to say, we're thankful that we had him in our life for 24 years. Many people lose children much younger. Yes, we wanted many more years with him, but we could have gotten less, and are very thankful we didn't.

There are even things about his final ITP battle that we are thankful for. The morning of his stroke was a whirlwind, but we're thankful he was at our house when it happened, and that he was physically able to text Donna, so she could run down and spend some alert time with him. We're also thankful that I happened to not be traveling for business that morning. I was right up the street when I found out about it, so I was able to see him while he could still communicate, and Donna wasn't left alone to deal with things. As bad as the situation was, he didn't really suffer, there was some discomfort, but he was not in severe pain. And finally, we're thankful for the support system we have, from all the friends and family that lived at the hospital with us, to Assa Abloy, who all the way up to the global CEO, supported us through this horrible phase of our lives.

There are a couple of key lessons we learned as we think back over Devin's short life. First, is to never give up on your child. The diagnosis of autism can knock you backward and leave you staggering, but all it means is that you have to be creative and try different things, and adjust the world around your child so all appreciate them for who they are. When Devin was four, or for that matter, eight, I would have never thought he would be into writing poetry, or singing in front of crowds. Donna tried everything she could think of with him, and these two stuck. If you are dealing with a similar diagnosis, don't give up, try everything, you never know what you will find. High functioning Autism is sad because your child knows they are different, and wants badly to make friends, but also, loves unconditionally, and brings joy to the world around them, without even knowing it.

The biggest lesson we learned was to be careful not to get complacent when you have a repeat medical issue. After they each had ITP a couple times, we became relaxed when we got the diagnosis. Had we any idea that it could be fatal, or had Devin's final bout been his first, as severe as it was, we would have certainly done things differently. All I can say is this… take the time to understand every aspect of any medical issue, know the possible risks, and advocate for your child.

Chapter 6

SIGNS

———

Some may say it's crazy, but we have been seeng some signs that Devin's spirit is still around us. We were in the hospital two weeks, and for another week after that, we did not go up the spiral staircase in our house. This leads to a small office above the kitchen, and is a place you could find Devin ahead of family gatherings, or during them if there was too much commotion. One evening, as we were watching TV, we heard the inkjet printer kick on and warm up on the upstairs computer. We went up there and the computer was turned on, and at the Google search page.

Everywhere we go, we hear his music. I met Kullen for lunch one day a few weeks after the celebration of life, and the background music was one of the Coldplay songs Devin sang. My dad and my brothers Brad and Chad came to visit one day, and as they pulled out of the house, the Elton John song was on the radio.

Within a couple months of us returning home from the hospital, nearly every single light bulb in the house – both porch bulbs, the bulbs in the master bathroom shower and vanity, and all over the living room – and the detached carport had to be replaced. Every time we head out in the car, we come across a falcon, sitting on a fence post, telephone pole, or tree branch, just looking at us as we pass by.

Our lake neighbors all went together and got us a nice white bench with a plaque in memory of Devin. Ron and Cheri, some other friends of ours from the lake got us a unique wind chime, it has a deeper pitch than most, and has a nice inscription on it. We put this and the bench together in our backyard that is like a park setting. It's between our carport, our house and the neighbors house, so little wind gets there, but still some days, we will hear his chime gonging from inside the house, and we think of him.

We noticed that there is a channel on Dish Network that now continiously plays movies Devin liked. Shows like "I Love You Man," for example. I was walking through Walmart and there was a huge bin of DVDs for $5. Right on top was the set of "Naked Gun" movies with Leslie Nielson, one of Devin's favorite comic actors.

Donna and I decided to get away in early December 2019. A change of scenery would be good. We went to the beach in Florida, but specifically a place where Devin had not been. We chose Destin, not far from where my brother Jeff lives with Tracy and Sierra. One of the days, while walking around the boardwalk at Fort Walton Beach, we went into a souvenir shop, and came across a picture magnet with a definition of the name Devin.

This was one of the few times we ever found one with his name spelled correctly – as usually we would find it spelled Devan or Devon. We put one of our favorite photos in it, the one from the Fish House the week before his ITP struck. Devin completely lived this definition of his name.

Photo magnet defining the name Devin

Devin has come to me a few times in dreams. In most cases, the interaction has been brief, and sometimes there is no dialogue. I'm not sure if this happens to you, but sometimes in my dreams I can't exactly tell where we are, but it might feel like my hometown, or somewhere else we lived.

12/17/2019. I was with a young Devin, like middle school age, at an event with bleachers. He was all smiles, and his voice was really squeaky. They had this robotic system that could find you. Not sure why. Seems like it was maybe a game or something. He bet me that if he would lay down it would not be able to find him. I challenged him to try sitting up first and then try laying down. So he ran ahead of me and sat by Celeste, a friend of his from back then. The machine was about to find him so I grabbed him and we ran to the other side of the bleachers and he laid down and it could not find him. We went and got some snacks.

12/29/2019. We were in a camper. Devin was about middle school age, and was talking to us. He was in bed and wanted a drink. His bed was power-adjustable, like a hospital bed. He asked for a Pepsi, but the only kind of Pepsi we had was diet, so he went with a Mr. Pibb instead. Donna and I both got kisses and hugs. While in this dream he was younger, it also felt like it was after his passing, because in the back of my mind I was ecstatic to see him, and was excited that I could call the insurance company and tell them never mind.

1/31/2020. Devin was younger, again about middle school age, in the breakfast nook area of our house in Smyrna, giving Kullen a hard time while he was trying to do his homework. Kullen would be concentrating, and Devin was laughing and jumping around, sticking his tongue out at Kullen, and trying to distract him.

2/4/2020. Donna and I were being lazy one morning, in what felt like our house on Coachlight Drive in Mascoutah. We were in bed. Devin was in the shower then came into our room. He was about eight years old at the time. He had a truck he built with Legos he wanted to show us. When he got in the room, he turned on the TV. He was all smiles. He didn't talk much, but when we asked questions, he would say "yep."

3/31/2020. Full dream about Devin as an adult (early twenties). He was at a clinic or therapy place and could have a visitor for an hour, but at the same time, it was open, like an apartment with a common area, for recreation and dining. The space was about 30 by 30 feet with a short wall between the two areas. Only dads were there this time. It felt like Donna was along but out in a lobby area.

Devin wasn't overly happy or sad when I got there. I got a huge hug when he first saw me. He began smiling after a while and got bouncy the longer I was there. He talked, but very little of anything I remember. I asked if he wanted something. He said after his blueberry pop tart. He offered me one. He ate Pop-Tarts and some other stuff. Then we sat and played a board game. Then we decided to head to another area and rest for a few minutes.

I was cleaning up our mess, and he walked ahead. I looked over, and he was in a full navy blue Adidas sweatsuit and white T-shirt. He had his music and white earbuds. He was smiling ear to ear. He was across the room near a wall, walking, with one arm up to the ceiling in his stutter-step gait as he giggled about something in the song he was hearing.

When we got to the other room we were sitting up high like on a short wall or something. He was on my right side. Other dads came in and sat right in front of us. One shook Devin's hand and I bumped elbows with the guy, in COVID-19 fashion, then Devin said "whoops" and hit like five pumps of hand sanitizer and laughed. He was sitting right by me, on my right side, like he did hundreds of times over the years. I could feel him there with me.

At the end, I was laying on a couch or bed, and he was sitting up on the edge of the bed. I asked what time I got there and he said a time that was later than it currently was. We figured out I had about 10 minutes left. I woke to the sound of Devin's wind chime going crazy in the back yard. I looked out, and there was hardly a breeze.

8/18/2020. We were in Freeburg at my parents' house, in the driveway. Devin was in his twenties, and his Grandma Judy was there. Devin gave me a huge hug, and I kept hugging till others complained it was their turn. While hugging him I told him it was my favorite thing in the whole world. He moved on and gave Donna a big hug, too. We started shooting baskets. As usual, we were playing horse and doing trick shots. This time, Bob Barker was announcing our shots, though. The backboard was on the end of the garage, and so sometimes when we would shoot, the ball would hit the end of the roof and miss the target. These would be the only shots Devin would miss.

One of my rebounds fell into a hole in the yard and shot out like a pinball and Devin caught it. We went inside for snacks, and he found a cereal called Fred's Yabba Dabba something or other, and was skipping around the kitchen laughing at the name. Donna grabbed my hand in her sleep, and I woke up.

There was also a time we believe Devin came to us, but not in a dream. On the one year anniversary of Devin's passing, a few friends and family members came to spend some time with us, as they knew we would be struggling. We spent time watching football and sitting outside looking at the lake. Around mid-afternoon, we all wrote messages on biodegradable balloons and carried them down toward the water. We took turns telling funny stories and talked about how much we miss him. Then we released the balloons.

Several were taking photos, but the one on the next page that Tracy took was the most amazing of them all. The balloons are the group of dots to the right side of the sun.

None of us saw the giant "D" in the sky while standing out there, but as we were going through photos, there was no mistaking it. We believe he was with us that afternoon.

D in the sky during the balloon release

Chapter 7

MOVING FORWARD

———

So… Now we find ourselves without one of the most wonderful people in the world. We are damaged goods, to say the least. But we must move forward. This is something you don't get over; you just learn to live through. We also find ourselves in clubs we never thought we would be in – The Compassionate Friends, for example. These folks reached out to us by sending a laminated copy of Devin's obituary to our house. We researched and found a local chapter in Breese, Illinois. This is a group therapy session, specific to people who have lost children, so they can all relate to the pain we are going through. We also participated in a grief share program through a church in Highland. This was good, too, but was for all kinds of loss, most of which were not children, but nonetheless, this helped us get through the holidays.

Can Good Come from This?

After twelve months of beating ourselves up, we have decided that what's best is to move forward, carrying the grief, so that we can have a positive influence on others. Donna has spent many hours on websites like the Platelet

Disorder Support Association[(M)] and some Facebook groups of parents who have lost a child, raising awareness that ITP can, in fact, kill you, and encouraging people to advocate for themselves – staying in the hospital as long as possible, and also sharing stories with people experiencing similar loss and grief.

We are not convinced that all the bug sprays required to tolerate life by the lake in the summer didn't at least contribute to how severe his final bout of ITP was. We are also not convinced that lithium combined with all his other medications, and with alcohol, didn't at least contribute to it, too. We are not sure there is any way to enact change in these areas, but want all to be aware there are concerns.

Our next mission is to start the process of changing the protocol for hospitals, to establish guidelines for dealing with ITP cases. There currently is no U.S. protocol stating minimum platelet levels required before a patient can leave the hospital, nor is there a requirement to do CT scans, regardless the platelet count or severity of other symptoms. In extreme cases like ours, where there is an active brain bleed, there is no protocol. They simply must do their best to follow normal ranges of platelets required to do things like craniotomy and splenectomy surgeries. We believe the protocols in these emergency situations should be based on the number of minutes since onset of the stroke, not on the platelet count, because, as we've seen, waiting for platelets to rise doesn't always work.

As parents, we would have appreciated a different approach. First, when there is a significant nose bleed – one that takes longer than five minutes to stop, for example – a CT scan needs to be done to ensure there is no internal bleeding. Second, when the patient presents with a massive brain bleed, and the required course of action is to open the skull to relieve pressure, there should be an absolute maximum waiting period, regardless the platelet count. All would understand that with low platelets the patient might not survive the surgery.

Is He Still Out There?

Since Devin's passing, we've done another thing that may seem crazy to some, and possibly contradictory to church. We have reached out to mediums, to attempt to connect with him, if he is still around, in spirit. We were referred to a couple mediums, who came across with some interesting comments, such as, a name Jack or Jackie (he was a patient of Dr. Jackie) and also a cowboy named John (Donna's step-dad, John, was from Texas). While these gave us a glimmer of hope, there was not overwhelming confidence in the reality of what we had heard.

In early April 2020, we had a reading with Suzanne Giesemann, a world-renowned evidential medium, over Zoom video conference. There were several key comments that came up, that gave us a true sense that his spirit is still around us, and he is doing well. Suzanne's comments are followed by what makes them interesting in parentheses:

- ➢ Mom is like a librarian (Donna worked in the Triad High School Library while Devin was a student there)

- ➢ Brother wants a tattoo of Devin's name (Kullen visited us the Wednesday before the reading, and standing in the kitchen, asked for a copy of Devin's signature, to be a template for a tattoo).

- ➢ A wind chime that we didn't have before he passed away is now ringing when it shouldn't (this is the chime from Ron and Cheri)

- ➢ He believes a chemical reaction with multiple doctors in the mix, and increasing doses caused the issue (had medicines from 3-4 doctors at the end, and one dose was doubled a week before the issue)

- ➢ Passing was mostly painless, but there was some pain around the rib cage and heart palpitations (His heart rate was around 180 beats per minute for several hours before the Craniotomy.)

- ➢ She saw him with earbuds in, and he wears them more than most. (Every minute he could, he would have his earbuds in, listening to music, and changing the volume constantly – even though he had speakers, he preferred his earbuds).

- ➢ He was big into movies (Devin loved to recite movie quotes, at just the right time, to get a laugh out of the group.).

➤ He was a loner who always wanted to please people, was judicious with words, but on his topics, would come alive. (He preferred to be alone. When together, you could see his face light up if you picked a topic he enjoyed – a movie – or a rap artist.).

➤ He remembers wrestling with dad and brother when he was young, also remembers camping and hiking when younger (recall the "get up on there" game I mentioned earlier).

➤ He senses that we are wanting to help others with similar issues now (this book, and Donna's work with the hospitals and websites)

We were astonished by the connection Suzanne had made. There were things she knew that no one knew, like the tattoo Kullen mentioned in the kitchen the week leading up to the reading, and the new wind chime that sounds at strange times. We were left with a sense of peace that he is in fact okay. Having reached this point, we decided we will not continue seeking connection in this world, but will put our focus on seeing him again in the next.

Keeping His Memory Alive…

Each time we gather with family and friends I we feel compelled to mention Devin. At major holidays like Thanksgiving and Christmas, we set a place for him at the table, and when we do a toast, we mention him.

When certain things happen that we know would have made him laugh, we are sure to mention it.

I mentioned earlier that Devin and I spent a lot of time in the Jeep. In early 2020, my friend Gary helped me out with a lettering project to customize it. We put one of Devin's many nicknames across the sides of the hood, and smaller, in memory of Devin Winter with his dates on the back. As you can see from the image below, he did another "almost professional" job. I also found a place online that lets you create custom tire covers, so had one made showing Devin's smiling face.

The Devster lettering by Gary

The Big Picture…

For years, we have had concerns about Devin's salvation. He was so black-and-white in his thinking that he struggled with church. Every day, he would stress if he had a bad thought, concerned that he was headed to hell. Eventually, we allowed him to stop going. As I was digging through emails, I came across one shortly after his cousin Zach was hit by a truck and left paralyzed. In this email, he asked me if Zach would have been better off if he didn't survive. In his words "well, assuming he didn't go to the hospital, he'd be going to heaven, so I, for one, wouldn't be grieving as much as feeling grateful because he'd be placed in God's hands." I'm so glad I came across this email. It is truly a blessing.

We never will be the same. We are broken, and I'm not sure it's possible to ever totally heal from this. The other day we took a Jeep ride around the lake, which Devin used to love to do. We stopped and sat on a bench. The lake was nice, but it was no longer wonderful, like it used to be. The lake has not changed. We have. I liken it to a scale from one to ten, with one being horrible, and ten being incredible, and now we have a bookend, so we will never feel anything above an eight. This is the life we now have, as we carry this loss with us and attempt to move forward. As we've spent time in grief counselling, I've been told to be careful with words like never. In the end, we will again be happy, and may be just as happy at points in time, it will just be a different type of happy, which doesn't make it not equal.

All that said, we will continue moving forward, albeit with much less joy and excitement than we once had in our lives.

Chapter 8

BLESSINGS

———

While we are moving forward, and while most of the time, there is limited joy and abundant sadness and hollow feelings, I would be remiss if I didn't point out some of the blessings we've encountered since his passing.

During our two weeks living with Devin in the ICU, Donna and I were talking and realized that regardless the final outcome (complete recovery, a life of profound handicap, or him passing away) our lives would change forever. We had visited a small church in Carlyle a few times over the 18 months or so that we lived there. Even though we were not members of Carlyle Christian Church and weren't even regular attendees, Pastor Josh saw the story of Devin and came to the hospital to pray for the family. Two weeks after Devin passed, we decided to become active in CCC. We began to go every week, and on New Years Eve, were baptized and became members. This is a non-denominational setting, with a group of fantastic, welcoming, caring people, focused on outreach to the local community. We are lucky we found them, and they are helping us through these difficult times.

A couple of months after the celebration of life, I asked my older brother, Darren, to look into Devin's computer that he had sold to Kullen's friend, Steve, to see if there were any poems, and Darren recovered nine.

You Shall Be Naked Henceforth
(A Katauta – 5/7/7 syllable counts)

If you stay naked,
It could be healthy for you
You should free yourself from clothes

Germaine Smokes Marijuana
(A Katauta – 5/7/7 syllable counts)

Canibus is great
His voice and lyrics are cool
His intelligence is high

The Misanthropy Inside Me
(A Sedoka – a pair of katuata)

I truly hate you
You lie to and steal from me
You beat me and insult me

You don't know the truth
You ask where evil comes from
But only you can be blamed

My Angry, Sad Self
(A Sedoka – a pair of katuata)

Laughter surrounds me
I'm too angry to make jokes
I'm continuing to pout

People are happy
I keep feeling sad often
There are times I have to cry

The Bittersweet Parents I Have

My parents are nice
They really do love me
They take me places
We watch movies together
And we play games too
I love and hate them at once
Why do I hate them?
Like lots of other people,
I don't like authority

I'm Sorry
(A Bussokusekika – a rare form, 5-7-5-7-7-7 syllables)

You say you love me
Even though I believe you,
This won't work for me

You keep hurting my feelings
Whenever we're together,
You mock me and are bossy

Get Over Here
(A Bussokusekika – a rare form, 5-7-5-7-7-7 syllables)

Sorcerers, ninjas,
Military officers,
Gods, and warriors
Here we have Mortal Kombat
It's the best video game
I've played it since my childhood

My Favorite Drink
(A Haiku)

Soda is awesome
Even though it's bad for me,
I drink lots of it

Great Parts of All People's Bodies
(A Tanka)

I have one of these
I enjoy looking at them
Mine relaxes me
Whenever standing tires me,
I use it for sitting down

I also did a password reset on Devin's Google Docs and found 25 more. What blessings these are. I only wish we had found them a few months earlier, so we could talk with him about what they mean, or what he was thinking about when he wrote them. I really miss the email exchanges we had when he would create a new poem.

How Unlikable You Are

Kindness, quietness,
Brightness, and humorousness
Qualities you wish
Came naturally to you
That I show effortlessly

Mitchell and I

Mitchell is abusive and overprotective
Many of his words are hurtful insults
Although he always keeps me company
He causes me to feel lonely unhappiness
In spite of his marvelous suggestions
He still hasn't helped me find contentment
In his presence I'm not in physical danger
Yet being awake isn't worth my energy
His main strength is constant awareness
If he were absolutely no part of my life
I wouldn't have communication or security

Truthfully his massive lack of humanity
I need to tolerate for typicality's sake

Ignorant Elimination

Dark shortness on top
A pair of sticks for lifting
In sadistic eyes
Explosions are like fireworks
A loving partner
Who ran and shot for decades
Until retirement
Supremely spiteful malice
Meets foreign glory and wealth

Swallowing for Pumps

Visibility
Doesn't remove the clearness
Merely transparent

Without a Tres

In terms of credit
Insufficient at the start
That which followed was treasured

What vanished was missed
Then delight was in demand
And apparent loot arrived

Phrasal Trickery

Dishonest deceit
The vocal alternative
To what should be heard
There's an unsuitable flow
Every word is mispronounced

Unexpected Sweetness

That's so surprising
All of it can still be found
Neither half has gone missing

Just pull it away
Disconnection leaves no leak
Also a thin attachment

Inharmonious Immorality

Those who are slothful
The unreasonable ones
Whoever avoids
Any troublesome hardness
Yet wants to possess,
Earn, achieve, own, and succeed
We're not one with them
Acknowledgement is evil
Because they have no honor

Consumable Riskiness

Hazardous wetness
Chemical dizziness may
Lead to slippery slickness

Where you end up next
You're capable of learning
Only after falling ill

It's a Cin

Age doesn't matter
What all the people's picks are
Unknown with no discussion

Swats, smacks, slams, and flicks
In spite of sounding harmful
Some are meant to be stared at

Who Says You Have To?

Being invited
And being forced don't unite
A separation
They are to be distinguished
One permits, one obliges

Wait, What Going?

There was some driving
One area occupied
Both guilt and concern present

Upsetting the Mourners

Inappropriate
Think outside of your own world
Celebratory
Don't let it pour all over
And we know your head is hot
But we don't need the fever

Much Rest for the Wealthy

The bed has a canopy
Can it be a tent?
Whose is it?

Egotistical Ranting

Inconsistency
Only others refer to
And the guilty ones
They try to defend themselves
But no one agrees with them

Harsh Tenderness

A sting, chap, or burn
A predictable outcome

On the contrary
Another result could be
Tame, soft, gentle friendliness

All Is Unsatisfactory

Before two and one
The strategic engagement
Accompanied by
The visual nostalgia
Each dimension was a thrill

Double the Calling

The stargur below
Driving a qin in reverse
Why'd you insult me?
What you said made me shiver
Or am I getting a drink?

Just Ignore It

The preferred manner
Currently negligible
A more proper style

In the Name of Smallness

The repulsiveness
Billions will be passed around
A unique version
No wrapping currently done

At least you're not vomiting
The top can be seen within

Ahead or Behind

An introduction
Uncertain, unsure, doubtful
Which one came to me?

Who's in Charge?

The puppet eats rolls
An aching and a falling
So historical
Obey, listen, heed, behave
Oh wait they're not of that sort

Impossible to Move Along

Not going forward
Hard, bumpy, rough, and rugged
That's the description
Confirmed by the messenger
Directional secrecy

Regrettable to Take

To avoid looking
Is a wisely polite choice
The domination
Sensibly seen as helpful
But still not worth enduring

Competitive Soullessness

We've started the game
One side meekly surrendered
Half their funds from work
Thousands of dollars received
Whether their rivals make cents
The other team are careless

Stay Focused or Go

No difficulty
Filthiness is adequate
Allow the air to pass through

Neither shut nor closed
The penetrability
Unsafe is the openness

Chapter 9
THANK YOU

———

Thank you, Devin, for changing me, for teaching me how to love, for teaching me to appreciate the simple things in life, like board games and movies, and for always smiling, even while miserable inside at times. Thank you for challenging me to confront my fears; without you, I never would have parasailed, ziplined, or been launched atop the Stratosphere. Thank you for the songs you sang so well, that I have now and can listen to anytime I want to hear your voice. And thank you for your poetry that so well shows the world how you struggled with thoughts, how you processed information, and how creative you were.

I miss you terribly and love you more than you ever knew.

Appendix 1

REFERENCES

——

A	https://www.cdc.gov/vaccinesafety/concerns/thimerosal/index.html
B	https://ghr.nlm.nih.gov/condition/autoimmune-lymphoproliferative-syndrome#definition
C	https://www.ncbi.nlm.nih.gov/pubmed/29911256
D	https://pubmed.ncbi.nlm.nih.gov/25663566/
E	Shenoy S, Arnold S, Chatila T, Response to steroid therapy in autism secondary to autoimmune lymphoproliferative syndrome: J Pediatrics. 2010 May, 136(5): 682-87.
F	https://www.hopkinsmedicine.org/health/conditions-and-diseases/idiopathic-thrombocytopenic-purpura
G	https://www.healthline.com/health/idiopathic-thrombocytopenic-purpura-itp#causes
H	IVIG https://lymphosign.com/doi/full/10.14785/lpsn-2014-0025?src=recsys
I	Rituxan http://chemocare.com/chemotherapy/drug-info/Rituxan.aspx
J	Winter D, Peppermint Rooster Review, Spring 2017; 5, p63.

K	Winter D, Peppermint Rooster Review, Spring 2017; 5, p64.
L	Winter D, Upon Arrival, Triumph. Pennsylvania: Eber & Wein; 2017. P 252.
M	https://pdsa.org/itp-warriors-donna-devin.html

Appendix 2

INDEX OF DEVIN'S POEMS

———

Appendix 3

ITP TIMELINE

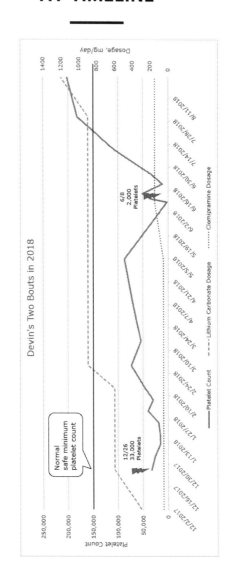

ITP Timeline – Devin's Bouts #2 and #3

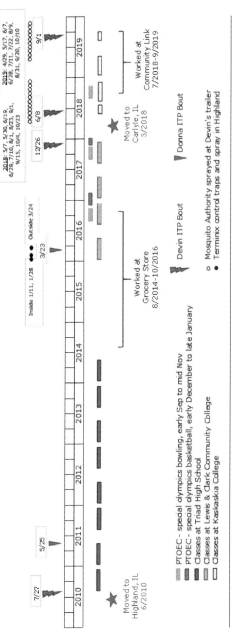

2019: 4/29, 5/17, 6/7, 6/28, 7/11, 7/22, 8/9, 8/31, 9/20, 10/10

9/1

2018: 5/7, 5/30, 6/19, 6/29, 7/10, 8/1, 8/23, 9/1, 9/15, 10/4, 10/23

6/8

12/26

Inside 1/11, 1/28

Outside 3/24

3/23

5/25

7/27

Worked at
Community Link
7/2018-9/2019

Moved to
Carlyle, IL
3/2018

Moved to
Highland, IL
6/2010

Worked at
Grocery Store
8/2014-10/2016

▶ Donna ITP Bout

▶ Devin ITP Bout

PTOEC - special olympics bowling, early Sep to mid Nov
PTOEC - special olympics basketball, early December to late January
Classes at Triad High School
Classes at Lewis & Clark Community College
Classes at Kaskaskia College

o Mosquito Authority sprayed at Devin's trailer
• Terminix control traps and spray in Highland

Note. Donna's platelets were 324,000 on 3/10/16, ruling out Terminix as a trigger

ITP Bout 12/2/17		
Date	Lithium mg/day	Clomipramine mg/day
12/2/17	300	50
1/24/18	600	50

ITP Bout 6/8/18		
Date	Lithium mg/day	Clomipramine mg/day
5/21/18	900	50
6/29/18	900	150

ITP Bout 9/1/19		
Date	Lithium mg/day	Clomipramine mg/day
7/15/19	600	150
8/12/19	900	150

Lithium doses as noted in doctors notes. Clomipramine doses from CVS records.

Made in the USA
Monee, IL
17 June 2021